A MARRIAGE MADE IN FOOTBALL

A MARRIAGE MADE IN FOOTBALL

The Story of Graham and Jane Hawkins

Kirstie Hawkins

Copyright © 2022 Kirstie Hawkins

All rights reserved.

ISBN-13: 9798839490499

Photographic and Artwork Acknowledgements

The author would like to thank the following for permission to reproduce photographs and images:

Bob Thomas Sports Photography via Getty Images
Louise Cobbold Art
Stoke Sentinel Newspaper
Blackburn Rovers Football Club
Jane Hawkins (personal photograph collection)
Denis Conyerd (personal photograph collection)

Cover art painting by Louise Cobbold:
Graham Hawkins in the dugout during his time as Wolverhampton Wanderers manager from a photograph by Bob Thomas Sports Photography via Getty Images

Contents

Foreword v

Introduction 1

1 Me Tarzan, You Jane 8

2 Harry the Horse 22

3 Bye Bye Black Country, Hello Lilywhites....................41

4 By Skill and Hard Work...59

5 A Brief Foray into the Fourth Division 73

6 A Gay Time at the Meadow 89

7 A Game of Two Halves..102

8 From Woore to War and Back Again 127

9 If You Marry a Footballer…You'll End Up in a Pub 143

10 Old School, New School 154

11 The Big 'C' is for Charity and Chicken....................174

Afterword 182

Eulogy 185

Bibliography 190

Tributes 192

Notes 194

Dedication

For Rich. Whilst we will have to get close to treble figures to enjoy the longevity of your parents' marriage, may ours be as happy.

For Lauren, Amy, Holly and Louisa. This is what GDad did.

Thanks to...

Jane Hawkins née Turner: this is Jane's book, this is Jane's story and without her blessing and patient responses to my hundreds of questions it wouldn't exist.

Dr Richard Hawkins: husband, best friend, football sports scientist at Manchester United since 2008, formerly of Sheffield United and West Bromwich Albion Football Clubs as well as The FA. He is also the author of The Official FA Guide to Fitness in Football, although he'd rather I mentioned his contributions to more academic sports science articles.

Uncle David (Turner): Jane's big brother, raconteur, immensely knowledgeable football (and many other sports for that matter) fan, good friend of Graham's.

Uncle Andrew (Hawkins): Graham's adored little brother and part-time football coach.

Professors Derek and David Siveter: twins, school football team-mates of Graham and life-long friends. Professors at Oxford and Leicester University respectively.

Terry Holder: school and Staffordshire Boys football team-mate and life-long friend of Graham. Successful newspaper entrepreneur.

Edward Skingsley: author of numerous books on Preston North End, possibly Graham's biggest fan outside immediate family.

Derek Fazackerley: dear friend to Graham. 671 appearances for Blackburn Rovers. Currently coach at Oxford United.

Jeff Kent: author of numerous books on Port Vale (and other topics).

Nigel Pearson: young player at Shrewsbury Town when Graham was Assistant Manager. Assistant Manager at West Bromwich Albion when Richard was Head of Fitness and Conditioning. Experienced football manager (currently manager of Bristol City) as well as legendary Sheffield Wednesday player 1987-1994.

David Harrison: Wolves fan, football journalist author of numerous books on football, loyal friend to Graham.

David Instone: football journalist author and publisher of numerous books on both Wolves and West Brom and very generous with his advice.

Jim Barron: goalkeeper, goalkeeping coach and Graham's assistant manager at Wolves.

Denis Conyerd: Wolves fan and Wolves physio recruited by Graham.

Michael Morrison: Graham's lawyer cum-friend, Manchester United fan.

Alf D'Arcy: talented amateur footballer, business owner, organiser of football tours and agent who recruited Graham (and many other former footballers) to managerial posts overseas.

Chris Green: author of Every Boy's Dream, book on youth development featuring input from Graham, raconteur extraordinaire, adviser on all things books and founder of Chris Green Media.

Jon Pither: cardiologist, founder of Elite Sports and later founder of PML, responsible for majority of heart screening of young elite football players and friend of Graham.

Jim Briden: Youth Development and Business Operations Manager at the EFL and friend of Graham.

Louise Cobbold: talented artist, renowned for her portraits of Wolves players from photographs, including the stunning painting on the cover of Graham whilst Wolves manager from an image by Bob Thomas Sports Photography, courtesy of Getty Images..

Boris Starling: great friend and always full of good advice. Talented author of gripping fiction and non-fiction of many genres, including sport.

Foreword

Judith Gates, June 2022

The footballing world is full of stories. Stories of games won and lost in final moments, penalties missed, managers sacked, deadline transfers, million pound deals. Yet what is rarely recorded, away from the glamour and the headlines, are the everyday stories of players and wives, couples and their families, living, sometimes in the glare of publicity, but, more often than not, living behind their own front doors, making decisions, raising children, contributing to their community, an integral, but sometimes overlooked, part of the footballing world.

In 'A Marriage Made in Football' Kirstie Hawkins opens the door to reveal the life of a family living in and through football. Her father-in-law, Graham Hawkins, was a professional footballer and later a football manager. Over a playing career spanning fifteen years he made over 500 first team appearances in the professional game, playing for Wolves, Preston North End, Blackburn Rovers and Port Vale. In his first season as a manager he led his team, Wolverhampton Wanderers, to promotion to the First Division, while his subsequent management career was in Bahrain. Latterly his commitment to the footballing world was as Head of Youth Development for the Football League. He truly devoted his professional life to the sport he loved.

And always by his side was his wife of almost fifty years, Jane. Together they raised two children. Together they faced the vagaries, challenges and joys of a life in the world of football. It wasn't always a glamorous life. Competing for a place in the first team led to enforced relocations. Corporate financial realities cut short a management career. Managing abroad uprooted the education of their children.

However, the joys of the sport outweighed the challenges. Together Graham and Jane navigated a complex life, in and out of the footballing limelight, maintaining always a strong sense of family alongside an ethical commitment to community.

The book is a tribute to one footballing family, but resonates with the lives of many others, my own included. Invariably away from the headlines, we live lives reflective of families of our era - until our paths intersect on key sporting issues of the day.

I am chair and co-founder of Head for Change, a recently formed charity committed to being part of the solution to sports-related brain injuries. We offer care and support to affected players and their families, engage internationally with the best brains in science to further much needed research, plus work diligently to promote awareness and education on the dangers of repetitive head impacts and concussions. My husband, Bill Gates, was a longtime defender for Middlesbrough FC. A contemporary of Graham Hawkins. Bill is now suffering from dementia, with a diagnosis of probable chronic traumatic encephalopathy (CTE), a neurodegenerative disease which is a direct consequence of blows to the head. I, too, have a marriage made in football.

Kirstie became aware of the work of Head for Change after reading that Tony Parkes, a former team-mate of Graham's at Blackburn Rovers, is now experiencing the devastating impact on him and his family of sports related dementia. Knowing of his lifetime commitment to charitable work, she and her husband, Dr Richard Hawkins, who also has a career in football, determined that it would be a fitting tribute to Graham if the proceeds from the sale of 'A Marriage Made in Football' were donated to Head for Change.

So, with sincere thanks to the Hawkins family, both for sharing their story and for their generosity, I, together with my colleagues at Head for Change, join in celebrating the life of Graham Hawkins; footballer, manager, coach and educator; husband, father and grandfather. Graham and Jane had 'A Marriage Made in Football'.

FOREWORD

Graham's life will be remembered. His legacy will live on through the players and families helped by the telling of his story.

A MARRIAGE MADE IN FOOTBALL

The beginning of Richard and Kirstie Hawkins' Marriage Made in Football, Florida 2018.

Introduction

At the time of writing, I have been married to football for three years, and 'involved' for six. As is the case for many a divorcée in the 21st century, I met husband Richard through a dating website. I did my homework on my potential love-match/psychotic serial killer prior to meeting him. Google revealed that he worked for Manchester United and had a PhD: he sounded glamorous and intelligent. Promising indeed. I liked football, I'd been to a few Sheffield Wednesday games over the years and I felt that it was a part of my Northern identity, a feature of my working class roots. Not that you'd know this on a first date, given the accent I cultivated to fit in with the posh kids at university. Going to the occasional football match, however, is a long way from marrying it. As the late Princess Diana so eloquently coined, I have learned in my time together with Richard that there are 'three of us in the marriage'. The partners of many ardent football fans may identify with the sentiment of the national sport as a mistress of sorts, but when football pays your wages, it's your master as well.

Richard was born into football. His Dad was Graham Hawkins, footballer, football manager and laterally Head of Youth Development at the EFL (English Football League, namely the Championship, Divisions One and Two being the leagues left after the divorce from the Premier League). Graham started out his working life as a teenage apprentice at Wolverhampton Wanderers in the sixties and spent two seasons as their manager in the eighties. I met Graham for the first and last time in June 2016, three months before he died aged just 70. He succumbed to a bout of pneumonia as the cancer treatment we thought had saved him, had decimated his immune system. Having met my soulmate late in life, not knowing his father felt like a huge gap. I'd lost my Mum four years prior to meeting Richard, and coming so soon in our blossoming relationship, attending Graham's funeral was a somewhat daunting experience. Just a couple of days after Graham's death, tens of thousands of football fans paid their respects with a minute's silence at Molineux. As the soundless 60 seconds ticked on, I watched Richard and his older brother Ian on the telly making a lonely walk across the pitch to place a wreath behind the goal, at a Wolves home game against Norwich. Blackburn fans had also marked Graham's passing with a minute's silence at their first home game after he died, and Preston North End similarly paid their respects to their former captain. Hundreds came to Graham's funeral. It was standing room only at the chapel, just as Wolverhampton's Express and Star reported. The wake was held at a swanky new hospitality suite at Molineux, which at 300 capacity, had just about enough space. Beloved by his family, Graham was also mourned by his football community.

The day Richard had said goodbye to his Dad in the hospital in Shrewsbury, he came home and bashed out the fireplace. He needed to do something and we'd never liked it. Graham's passing left a big hole in many ways. As I got to know Richard's family at subsequent events, Graham's absence was always marked and clearly deeply felt. Granddaughter Holly, aged just 14 when her 'GDad' died, remembers catching her breath just before going on stage to perform at her dance show, spotting an empty seat in the audience next to her cousin Amy. She treasures the screenshot of the text message her Grandad had sent her a couple of months earlier, saying how excited he was to come to the show, finishing with 'GMa toLd mE to SenD tHis', the sporadic capitals an in-joke between the generations. Two years' later wife Jane, normally giving few signs of her own grief, always more concerned about her sons' or granddaughters' welfare, had a quiet cry at our intimate wedding in Florida that she would have loved to have shared with Graham.

As well as wishing I'd been able to get to know Graham as well as I have my wonderful mother-in-law Jane, I was always curious about Jane and Graham's marriage. They had met when they were both aged sweet 16 and remained happy and in love throughout. No small feat. I'd clocked a small wooden plaque hanging in Jane's kitchen with the message: 'Every love story is beautiful, but ours is my favourite', and wanted to understand how that sentiment could last a lifetime. I was

INTRODUCTION

also curious about Graham's football career - how did that fit in with a long and happy marriage? For a footballer or a football manager, weekends mean work and the off-season is the only time available for holiday and extended family time, which basically means that only the month of June is free, as pre-season training starts up again in July. The football calendar has no regard for weekend plans or school holidays, and anyone married to football will tell you that if your partner does get a day off work, they'll be watching it. There is always training on Christmas Day. Well, maybe the fixtures might fall favourably for one or two Christmas Days off over a lifetime.

The obituaries talked about Graham being unique in that he had played, scouted and managed his childhood club, but what happened after that? On the face of it, he'd been a successful manager, achieving promotion to the top flight at his first attempt in his first ever managerial position. His sacking was attributed to a familiar story of a lack of funds to buy the players needed to compete in the First Division rather than any weakness as a manager, so why had he not continued? I knew the family had moved out to Bahrain for a few years, that Graham had managed football teams there, but why not in England? Jane hadn't wanted to go to Molineux when Ian and Richard laid their wreath - why was that? She'd been at every home game supporting Graham when he was manager there. Richard had hinted that his Dad's second season as Wolves manager had been difficult - maybe that was it.

When the country went into lockdown in March 2020, I worried about Jane. Months of solitude loomed for her, and none of us had any idea when it would all end. She had coped valiantly after losing her husband, socialising with her wide circle of friends and family, but with the country facing a killer pandemic, she would be home alone indefinitely. We had become close; having married Richard she'd adopted me as well as my two sons. I think maybe my two cherubs remind her of her time as a Mum of two boys. It's a two-way thing: the little things Jane does for me remind me very much of how my Mum was - always thoughtful and kind. It wasn't long after the kids got sent home from school indefinitely in March 2020 that I was struck by the idea of writing Graham and Jane's story as a way of entertaining Jane, but also for me to get to know more about Graham. Compared to many, I wasn't too badly placed for home-schooling. I was at home, 40,000 words into a first attempt at a novel, set in 1970. I was already a bit stuck, and having the kids around wasn't helping the creative juices to flow. I had a need to occupy my mind with something that would fit around the kids. I'd occasionally mused that it would be great if my talented writer friend Boris Starling would pen Graham's story, but hey, why not me?

Our footballers are much maligned. In April 2020, shortly after the country shut-down amidst the early horrors of COVID-19, the then Health Secretary Matt Hancock decided that they should be singled out to 'take a pay cut and play their part', making no suggestion that any other high earners should make such a sacrifice. In 2021, as England's national team prepared for the delayed Euro 2020 tournament, Home Secretary Priti Patel was happy for supporters to boo their national team for making a stand against racism. Typically, sections of the English press portray footballers as unintelligent, pampered and fickle, seeking to set them apart from their working class supporters. Qualities such as loyalty, integrity, honesty, humility, hard-work and generosity, all relevant to a team's collective success, are typically ignored; I guess those stories don't sell as well as the wine, women and song scandals. Maybe this story won't sell either, but I'm ready for that: so long as Jane and Richard are happy with it, that's enough.

Graham signed for his beloved Wolverhampton Wanderers aged 16, making his first-team debut aged 18. He went on to manage Wolves, securing promotion to the top flight in his first season aged just 36. These were the glory moments, the moments about which much is written in books and in newspapers from the time, but Graham's working life spanned almost half a century, of which his time playing and managing Wolverhampton Wanderers Football Club makes up seven years. Most of Graham's life in football was well away from the huge salaries and glamour of the top flight. At his second club, Preston North End, he was a much admired captain. His third club was Blackburn and there is at least one 40-something in the North West named Graham after his father admired the strength and

INTRODUCTION

steeliness of the tall, handsome blonde centre back in the seventies. Graham made 502 first team appearances over a playing career of 15 years, and could have played for longer if his last club, Port Vale, hadn't prevented him in doing so by refusing to release his playing license over a contract dispute. He tried a few different jobs along the way, including running the ubiquitous pub, but always came back to football, not for the glory, definitely not for the money, but for love of the game, his craft. Graham and Jane's story is not about vast wealth or scandal, but how passion for the beautiful game brought both tough challenges and wonderful experiences. It is for Jane, it is our lockdown project, it is for their four granddaughters, so they and their children can have a record of 'what grandad did', but it is also for me. As a result of speaking to some of Graham's many friends together with a wealth of Emails from Jane who patiently answered all my questions as well as unearthing a wealth of memorabilia, photo albums, family home videos, DVDs of Preston North End, I now have a much deeper understanding of my husband's late father. Uncovering his story has been a joyous voyage of discovery of both a footballer and a gentleman.

I am not a football writer, and have not spent my life watching, talking and dreaming football. I am late to this game. Before meeting Richard, I had an interest somewhat more elevated than the average 40-something female, but I recognise that this falls a long way short of the qualifications required to write a book on the topic. My Auntie tells me that my great-uncle Billy Sellars was a professional footballer in the 1920s and 1930s, although other than his entry in Wikipedia and tales of his wife being treated to diamonds, I don't know really anything about him. Post meeting Richard, I have watched a lot of football, and talked a lot about football although I am yet to dream about football. I do not have the back catalogue of the average serious 40-something football fan, but some catching up has taken place. In the course of researching Graham and Jane's story, I have spoken to some wonderful people who know a lot about football, I have read some books written by people who have devoted their lives to watching and writing about football and I now consider myself reasonably well-informed about what it's like to be married to football.

Jane was my primary source, however although she has probably watched considerably more football than your average football fan, Graham's work was not something they discussed at length at the dinner table. For Jane and Graham, home life was the better for being a haven away from football, particularly when times on the terraces got tough. To help me get some perspective on Graham's life in football, Jane introduced me to many of Graham's friends and colleagues who all jumped at the chance to talk about their dear friend. As well as proper football people, I've also been helped along by proper football writers, and what a lovely bunch they are too - despite not knowing me from Adam and the fact that I have brazenly attempted to write a kind of football book with no proper qualifications, they have been nothing but supportive, encouraging and helpful.

INTRODUCTION

South Staffordshire Schoolboys 1959. Back row L to R: Mr Jackson (coach), MaCleod, Derek Siveter (of the Siveter twins), Knight, Challenor, Young Graham, Shuker. Front row L to R: Bailey, future England player Allan 'Sniffer' Clarke, Cox, Bellingham, Cartwright, Dams. Thanks to Derek Siveter for the cast list.

1 Me Tarzan, You Jane

1946 – 1962

The heroes of our story, Jane and Graham, both arrived in the world in 1946, the same year as one of the world's most famous footballers, George Best, although I reference Best merely to place Graham in his footballing era. Jane arrived first on 22nd February, at 463 Cannock Road, Wolverhampton. Graham was born some 11 days later at 10 Castle Street, Darlaston. Both Jane and Graham were born at home, as most babies were back then, a couple of years shy of the founding of the NHS in July 1948. Jane would stay at Cannock Road until she left to marry; Graham and his family moved just once, from a two-up two-down terraced house to a larger council house a mile north, in Wingate Road, Bentley. They would grow up just four miles apart, before meeting and falling in love aged 16. Theirs is a love story that lasted a lifetime, took them on journeys with at least as many highs and lows as ninety minutes on a football pitch.

World War Two was over when our couple was born, but the country was still reeling from the devastation caused by the years of fighting and Luftwaffe bombing raids. Jane and Graham spent their childhood in the post-war years, characterised by the dismantling of the British Empire and a focus on rebuilding a heavily bombed nation. Nevertheless, Wolverhampton had been spared some of the worst bombing raids, with German attempts to bomb Britain's munitions factories in the Midlands predominantly hitting Birmingham and Coventry. The football league had been suspended after the outbreak of war in 1939, with games resuming for the season of 1946/7 - just a few months after Graham and Jane were born. Liverpool topped the league that season, with Manchester United and Wolverhampton Wanderers just a point behind in second and third place respectively.

ME TARZAN, YOU JANE

The post-war period saw both my husband Richard's employer of 15 seasons and counting, Manchester United, and Wolves benefit from the fruits of their youth development under Matt Busby (Manchester United manager 1945-69) and Stan Cullis (Wolves manager 1948-64), affectionately known as Busby's Babes and Cullis' Cubs. Himself a Cullis Cub, Graham was heavily influenced by the legendary Wolves manager and in turn shaped son Richard's approach to youth development in his footballing career; I believe that it is no coincidence that Richard finds himself in a club with a legendary Academy and strong focus on home-grown talent.

When Jane and Graham were growing up, most homes did not have a television set and watching the local team from the terraces was a rite of passage for most working class men and their sons: Jane's father and brothers together with Graham and his Dad were no exception. Crowds at Molineux were regularly over 40,000. 'Where we lived we could hear the Molineux Roar when we were in the back garden, and my Dad would chat to the fans walking back home past our house,' Jane recalls. Even the reserves drew crowds of a few thousand, especially when playing against Manchester United. Jane's older brother David would regularly go and watch the Wolves reserves team play in what was then the Central League and remembers they were a particularly good side. Under Stan Cullis, Wolves established themselves as one of the best teams in the country, winning The FA Cup twice. 1954 saw Wolves become First Division champions for the first time in their history and they went on to win again in 1958 and 1959 as well as finish in the top three 12 times under Cullis. The team of Graham's boyhood were flying high in the fifties in the Cullis 'Golden Era'.

In 1953, Wolves were one of the first teams to invest in floodlights and subsequently hosted a number of night-time friendlies against international teams, including a famous match in 1954 against Hungarian champions Budapest Honvéd. Cullis said at the time: 'the whole future of football in Britain depends on our ability to face the challenge from abroad' and 'although I am in a minority I am sure we would be wise to have more games screened live. Television offers an opportunity not seen in all soccer's history, a whole new source of revenue, a vast sum which must make a considerable impact on the game.' Cullis was not wrong there. Inspired by the Wolves-Honvéd game, journalists from French sporting newspaper L'Équipe proposed a European Cup and it was duly born the following year, albeit The FA banned English champions Chelsea from participating on the basis it would interfere with the domestic league. Tensions between English and European football associations are nothing new, it would seem.

Richard's Uncle David, Jane's brother, remembers the Hungarians visiting the Wolves, not long after beating the England team: 'Yes I went to that game: it was very foggy, a miserable evening and the pitch, like it was in those days, was absolutely bog deep. Well they got off to a flying start, with their little short passes, and they actually went into a two-nothing lead, but the power of the Wolves team, they couldn't handle our big players and the big ball down the middle and in the second half we just mullered 'em. Three goals, to win 3-2, and they couldn't understand what was happening after they'd come and thumped the international team on Wembley, but they hadn't reckoned with Stan Cullis' boys because nearly everybody was over six foot, and they just used to get stuck in. The only exception was Hancocks - he was tiny, he was about five foot five, and he could hit the ball like a bullet. They just completely over-powered them.' Incidentally, Johnny Hancocks, former England international, went to work in an iron founders when his playing career ended, until he retired aged 60. Different times indeed.

The floodlights, whilst providing evening entertainment for David, were not without controversy. In 1956 they earned Molineux a visit from Jimmy Guthrie, the Players' Union chairman. The union had been campaigning for many years to lift the players' wage cap and they felt that players should be getting paid over-time for the night-time friendly games. After a meeting with Wolves' captain Billy Wright, the Wolves' players backed their union and went on strike, causing the cancellation of a scheduled match against Spanish team, Bilbao. Guthrie wasn't the only one perturbed by the prospect of night games under floodlights. In October 1956, Wolves fan Ernest Ward was also protesting: 'I might be 76 years' old, but I have plenty of fight.' He went on, 'It would be quite impossible for me to attend on Saturday nights. I consider the directors to have a contract with season ticket holders which they cannot legally lay on one side.' Progressive Cullis was unrepentant: 'Perhaps the loss of Mr Ward might be offset by the attendance of a few amateurs who play football on a Saturday afternoon.'

Jane, older brother David and younger brother Robert grew up in the shadow of Molineux, but in relative affluence. Dad Samuel's main occupation was running the coal delivery business that his father, Jane's grandfather, also Samuel, had started. Jane has a wonderful photograph of both Samuels together with their new coal truck, bought to replace their horse and cart, in a book of Victorian images of Wolverhampton. Business boomed as almost every home was powered by coal back in the forties and fifties. Dad, Samuel Robertson Turner, was a popular man about town, always making people laugh with his jokes. He met Jane's Mum, Muriel Irene Woodhead when she worked as a barmaid in the Newbridge pub on Tettenhall Road in Wolverhampton. Muriel had worked as a bookbinder previously, reportedly sacked for 'laughing too much' and the two of them shared a similar outlook on life, always seeing the funny side, an approach to life they passed on to their children. They fell in love but before they could marry, Samuel was in the somewhat sticky situation of having a wife already.

Samuel had married Jessie Mansell, an amateur opera singer, in August 1934 when he was 27, but it wasn't a happy marriage and they separated. Jane was led to believe that her father's first wife was somewhat dramatic and prone to violent outbursts. This was confirmed by one of Jessie's granddaughters who got in touch with Jane decades later, when researching her family tree. Obtaining a divorce in the 1930s was not easy. Prior to the Matrimonial Causes Act of 1937, adultery was the only legal reason a divorce could be granted. Once Samuel had decided to marry Muriel in 1942, he set the wheels in motion, and after waiting the required two years to satisfy the new divorce grounds of desertion, he finally got his freedom to remarry in October 1944. They duly wed on the first of November 1944 at the beautiful Wesleyan Methodist Chapel on Darlington Street in the centre of Wolverhampton. Samuel (37) and Muriel (30) were relatively old for starting out married life back then, but second time around proved to be a happy union for them both.

Samuel and Muriel's first child, David, wasn't prepared to wait for Samuel's divorce and arrived in July 1944, a babe in arms when his parents wed. David was just 19 months old when middle child Jane came along, and little brother Robert was born when Jane was four. According to Muriel, David and Jane were sent into a panic tidying all their toys away in case the newcomer 'messed' with them. Jane was shy as a young girl, happy to let her older, outgoing brother take the lead. David says: 'I can remember that when Jane was very little, she was very slow to talk because it was me that was asking for everything for her: "Can I have an ice-cream and one for Jane and so on?".' David jokes that he was knocked down the pecking order when his siblings arrived: 'I was always in trouble and she never was, you get the picture and it never changed - and it got a lot worse when Bob came along.' Jane's childhood in Cannock Road was a happy time growing up with her two brothers. Unlike most homes of the era, their three-bedroomed semi-detached house had its own bathroom and toilet, albeit an outside one. 'With Dad delivering coal to other businesses we never ran out of food - so fortunate.' Jane remembers.

As well as her two brothers, Jane also grew up living with mother Muriel's sister, Auntie Dot. After Muriel and Dot's father, Jane's maternal grandfather, Archibald, had died in 1956, Auntie Dot, being on her own, had moved in with the Turner family in Cannock Road. Samuel, Jane's father, owned the house they lived in (463), as well as the attached semi next door (461). Samuel initially rented out 461 to a retired couple, but the wife died leaving her husband living in the house alone. In order to accommodate his sister-in-law Dot, Samuel agreed with his tenant that he would knock through the two houses, partitioning off the former living room of 461 to create an annexe for Auntie Dot, and she became a part of the Turner household. The only minor complaint Dot had, was that her neighbour, Jim Matthews, liked a drink or two on the weekend, and she would hear him stumbling upstairs after a night in the pub. Dot never married, but was very much welcomed into the Turner clan, as were sisters Peggy and Mary, friends of mother Muriel who had also never married, and who feature on many family photos. Jane and her brothers were thus awash with doting aunts. Peggy would bemoan her lack of marriage proposals, but young David's offer to marry her when he grew up ensured eternal love. Jane remembers many a happy hour playing cards with the band of merry single ladies and pillow cases brimming with Christmas gifts for all of the children.

Like many families in the fifties, the Turners were regular church-goers, and Samuel's bass tones were much appreciated at hymn-time by his daughter. The family became close to the vicar - Jane remembers him joining the family to watch an FA Cup Final on their new television (acquired by Samuel to watch Queen Elizabeth's coronation in 1953). The church also provided social opportunities for Jane at the youth club held in the Bushbury Parish Church they attended, 'The Good Shepherd', where she would go to listen to records with her friends. Jane and her brothers happily found their own entertainment and music played a big part of their lives, a love passed on by both Jane and Graham to their sons. 'I loved my dolls, pram and house, dressing up, playing board games and making up games with my brothers. Christmas was always wonderful with presents, food and Dad making us laugh and singing,' says Jane. Brother David remembers being in the back garden with Jane and Robert, as Samuel performed operas for them from an upstairs window, using his box of wigs and outfits to switch characters. Samuel was a member of the Amateur Operatic Society and performed Gilbert and Sullivan comic operas at the Grand Theatre on Lichfield Street in Wolverhampton. Jane shared a love of the D'Oyly Carte (British light opera company that toured until 1982) with her Dad and they would go together to watch them perform operettas. Both David and Robert were football fans - as the older boy, David was the first to start going aged just ten, taking in games like the Honvéd clash. He recalls: 'Of course, that was the first year I started to go - they had a place called the kids' pen and Ernie Barnes who lived two doors away from us then, he used to take me, put me in there and meet me afterwards, you know. But not always, I didn't always used to stay in there, I used to get out and get in the North Bank with all the ruffians, as you would expect me to do anyway, Kirstie.'

A MARRIAGE MADE IN FOOTBALL

Graham's childhood was much less affluent than that of his future wife, and Jane remembers his mother, Ida, often went without food in order to feed her children. Ida was a kindly, happy soul - Graham's childhood friend David Siveter, remembers her 'hearty laugh'. In contrast, Graham's father Ernest could be tough on Graham and was ambitious for his son. He spent his working life as a die miller at Garrington's, a forging works in Darlaston, just to the east of Wolverhampton. Decades before any minimum wage, Ernest worked piecemeal, ie he got paid for what he produced, working alternate shifts of six in the morning to two o'clock in the afternoon one week then two o'clock to ten at night the following week. With just two bedrooms in their house in Castle Street, Graham shared a bedroom with his two sisters with a sheet hung from the ceiling to divide the space. There was an outhouse for washing both clothes and filling the tin bath and a row of toilets across a yard serviced the Hawkinses and their neighbours. 'I think I only went a couple of times to the toilet when Graham lived there - everyone knew where you were going,' Jane remembers with a shudder.

Ernest Norman Hawkins and Ida Mary Skitt married in 1935 when Ernest was 25 and Ida just 17, shortly before giving birth to their first son, Ernie in the same year. Graham and Jane would never meet Ernie as he tragically drowned when just seven years old in the canal near Ernest's workplace at Garrington's. A local youth, known to have learning difficulties, ran to tell Ernest about the tragedy, but was not able to shed any light on how little Ernie ended up in the canal. Years later, Graham and Jane would visit Ernie's gravestone and found that flowers were regularly lain by a mystery mourner, but they never found out who it was or whether or not they knew anything about what happened to Ernie. I can't imagine the heartbreak Ernest and Ida must have felt over losing their young son so tragically - the pain must have borne heavily on them, especially in the four years it took before Ida gave birth to her oldest surviving child, Graham. Despite suffering many miscarriages over the years, Ida went on to raise four children, Graham's first sister Maureen was born in 1950 when Graham was four, his second sister Susan arrived four years later in 1954 and finally Andrew was born in 1962 when Graham was 16 and their mother Ida 44 - just a few months before Graham first met Jane. With the new arrival, space was even tighter for the Hawkins family and it was a great relief for all the family when they moved to their three-bedroomed semi-detached council house a couple of miles away in Wingate Road, Bentley in 1964. Andrew has many happy memories of his talented big brother: 'I remember when he had his first car, I think it was a Ford Anglia. In Wingate road there was a large patch of grass and gravel with a slide and roundabout on it were all the kids from the area used to play football and cricket and Graham would park his car on it at night. He would sit me on his lap while he was parking the car up and I would think I was steering it.' Andrew also remembers a brother who kept his feet firmly on the ground at all times: 'Can I just say that Graham never forgot were he came from, a poor but humble upbringing, on a council estate in Darlaston and Bentley. When he was in the area he would drive around where he was brought up and notice all the changes that had happened.'

Graham's first school was Addenbrooke Street Primary, a short walk from home in Castle Street, and he was followed there by his two younger sisters. Through playing football for the school team, Graham was also selected to play alongside boys from other primary schools in a combined 'Darlaston Boys' team, where he met lifelong friends, twins Derek and David Siveter. Graham and the twins' fathers became friends through supporting their boys on the football pitch. In an Email to David in 2015, Graham reminisced, 'Remember your Dad and my Dad arriving at the football matches and shouting, "Herd 'em up and move them out!"?!' Derek helpfully explained to me that this was a quote from a popular sixties TV series, 'Rawhide', featuring Clint Eastwood as a cattle herder, with Ernie using it to mean 'stop the attack and move up the field!'. As well as Darlaston Boys, Graham and the twins were subsequently selected to play in the South East Staffordshire team. They were in fine company, playing with Allan Clarke in the 1958/59 SE Staffs team, who went on to play for First Division Champions Leeds United (via Walsall) as well as getting 19 caps for England. Proving the small and inter-connected world of football, Allan Clarke's little brother, Wayne Clarke, would go on to play for Wolves under Graham as manager.

Secondary state education in 1958 meant either grammar school for the lucky few who passed the 11+, or a secondary modern school for a more vocational study programme. Graham and the twins didn't pass the 11+ exam, as was common for the vast majority of children in the Wolverhampton area of that time - the dearth of grammar schools meant that the odds were stacked against them. They all went on to Slater Street Secondary Modern Boys School from the age of 11. The Siveter twins recall that Slater Street was 'a left-over from Victorian times, with the cane and other forms of corporal punishment much in evidence'. The local council, recognising the disadvantages, sought to address the lack of educational opportunities in the area and devised a 13+ exam to provide a form of grammar school education for those deemed to have missed out. Graham and the twins passed the exam and were all happy to escape Slater Street and move to another school, Wednesbury Technical School. 'This represented our chance to escape from the normal job progression of young men in the Black Country - a job in local industry.' Indeed both Derek and David went on to become academics, latterly Professors at Oxford and Leicester Universities respectively - not bad for a couple of boys who failed their 11+.

Wednesbury Technical School for Boys was situated on Holyhead Road, a couple of miles away from Castle Street. All the boys who had passed the 13+ were in the one class, 4T. It was here that Graham was introduced to basketball by his PE Teacher, Mr Pitt. The Siveter twins also became skilled basketball players - their school team won the South East Staffordshire League on more than one occasion, and Graham was selected as captain for the 1961/1962 season. Graham would always favour football, though, when a choice had to be made. An avid football fan, father Ernest always pushed Graham's footballing talent, seeing it as a way that Graham could enjoy a life more prosperous than his own.

In 1960, Wednesbury Technical School merged with Wednesbury Commercial College, and for his final year of school, Graham travelled a couple of miles to a temporary school site on Wood Green Road, whilst a new building was being finished as the intended home of what would later become Darlaston Grammar. As a result of the merger, Graham met good friend Terry Holder and they joined forces on the school football team coached by teacher Mr Wright, enjoying much success. Terry remembers: 'Our school football team was top notch and we played every Saturday morning against other schools and usually won.' Graham continued to play basketball, as did the Siveter twins and they persuaded Terry to join them on the team, but despite the best efforts of Mr Pitt as well as the school's headmaster, Mr Donithorn, to get the boys to focus purely on basketball, football remained Graham's first love. Graham and Terry would also play in a local men's football league in the afternoon, for Willenhall Torch, a club formed by the Salvation Army, excellent preparation for the physical challenges of the adult game for those who avoided injury.

Graham and Terry were selected to play for Staffordshire Boys in the 1960/61 season and they also got games with the Birmingham Boys' team. Games were played on a Wednesday afternoon, and the boys had the honour of being taken there by the headmaster himself, Mr Donithorn. Graham played centre half for the school team, but full back for Staffordshire Boys. Terry reminisced about their time playing together: 'Graham used to come forward for corners and, as the corner taker, I put the ball where I knew he would be with many goals as a result. Happy days!' A defensive player, Graham scored just ten goals in his first team professional career, and at least one of these was a headed match-winner from a set piece (August 1970, Preston North End V Wrexham).

It was on one of these Wednesday afternoons that the schoolboys were spotted by Wolverhampton Wanderers' scouts who subsequently came to watch the boys the following week in a school match. Graham and Terry were then invited to train at Castlecroft, the Wolves' training ground in the west of Wolverhampton, over seven miles from Graham's home in Castle Street. 'This meant an early meal after school and two buses,' Terry recalls, 'It was a tough schedule and football was a very physical game in those days. Graham was a strong boy and he knew it was his big chance. His father was 110% behind him.' Over six feet tall, Graham was the kind of player Cullis liked.

A MARRIAGE MADE IN FOOTBALL

Chatting with Clive Corbettt (Out of Darkness: History of Wolves 1977 - 1990) about his time as an apprentice, Graham spoke about how important Wolves were to him: 'A bus ride from Darlaston, paid my two shillings or whatever to get on to the South Bank. I'd arrive three hours early with my sandwiches and then wait for kick-off. Later I went training there and ended up playing with some of my heroes. There was a squad of about 40 and five teams at Wolves at that time. The first team players treated you with respect and I never heard any swear words. It was my club. I felt comfortable, and the discipline, work ethic and principles of Stan Cullis stuck with me all my life. It's fair to say I've got a great affiliation with Wolves, which has never waned.' Cullis was a Wolves man through and through, a player from 1934 through to 1947 when he retired due to injury, taking up the post of assistant manager before taking the top job a year later. Cullis made 12 appearances for England. In a match against Germany in 1938 he was the only English player to refuse to give the Nazi salute and was subsequently dropped from the team - a principled man for whom Graham had the utmost respect and admiration.

Terry's father felt differently about the opportunity Wolves represented, and encouraged his son to stay on at school rather than pursuing a footballing career. Like the Siveter twins, Terry also went on to have a successful career, ultimately owning his own newspaper (Wolverhampton Ad News) together with fellow school-pal, Phil Radburn. Graham didn't totally give up on his schooling, however, as he knew that he had to think of his life beyond football. Always one to plan ahead, after signing up to Wolves, he continued to study at college in the evenings, going on to pass his 'O' Levels in maths and biology.

Graham spent most of his free-time playing football, but also enjoyed socialising with his friends. As a school boy he would spend time at the youth club and on camping weekends with his friends - Derek and David Siveter remember a fishing trip to the River Avon, near Evesham, where they camped for several days. The boys would graduate to regular Saturday nights out at the local dances, at the Regent Club, Ship and Rainbow on Dudley Road in the south of Wolverhampton as well as the Tech (school) dance. It would be Jane's love of music and dancing, rather than Graham's love of football, that would first bring Jane and Graham together. Jane's big brother David, still dancing now with Jane when an occasion presents itself, would be Jane's first partner and David's love of football (and indeed sport in general) sealed a great friendship between the two men.

Whilst Jane and Graham were just 16 when they met, they had both already left school and started their working lives, earning money and becoming independent. Jane left school aged 15, spent six months in Queens Business College in the centre of Wolverhampton, studying typing, shorthand and book-keeping before starting work at Henry Meadows Ltd, a five minute walk from home. An interview with Mr Bennett, the Managing Director and also one of Samuel Turner's customers secured the position. Jane's duties involved working in the post-room, administrative tasks and she particularly enjoyed manning the switchboard.

Jane and Graham had their first encounter in October 1962, at the Regent Club in Wolverhampton. The austerity of the post-war years was over and the sixties were starting to swing. Britain was regaining its cool, as the Beatles released their first single, Love Me Do and The Rolling Stones played their first gig at the Marquee club in London. Jane had already been on dates with two of Graham's fellow Wolves team-mates David Woodfield ('the first cab off the rank', as brother David puts it) and Bobby Thomson. Jane had caught Graham's eye, but he knew that he'd have to work on his dancing to attract Jane's attention, and so recruited a former date, Helen, to help him learn to jive. It would be two months later that his efforts would be rewarded, on 27 December 1962. It might have been Graham's fancy footwork to Dream Baby by Roy Orbison or possibly The Night has a Thousand Eyes by Bobby Vee that won Jane over, but whichever song turned Jane's head, the music would continue to play for them for many years.

When Jane and Graham started to date, Britain was in the midst of the coldest winter since the eighteenth century: the 'Big Freeze' - so cold that the sea froze in the English Channel in places. Football matches had been cancelled across the country, with Wolves' last match taking place on 15 December 1962 against Manchester City (a 3-3 draw). Graham was yet to make his first team debut, but was playing regularly at the training ground at Castlecroft in either the youth or reserve teams in the Central League. Wolves wouldn't play again until 19 January 1963, meaning that instead of the usual congested fixture list over the Christmas break, Graham was free to focus on courting the pretty girl who had caught his eye on the dance floor. As a rule, football schedules don't leave much time for dating.

Having secured just the one dance with Jane, on closing time at 11pm Graham gallantly accompanied Jane to her bus-stop before inviting her to the cinema the following evening, a Friday night. The young couple went to see Tarzan Goes to India at the ABC Cinema on the corner of Garrick and Bilston Streets in Wolverhampton. The connection was made, there would be many more dates, with the swarthy footballer charming his beautiful date with the immortal lines, 'Me Tarzan, You Jane'.

Jane and Graham on their wedding day, 1967.

2 Harry the Horse

1962 – 1967

If the fifties were Wolverhampton's golden era of football, then the sixties were England's time, culminating in the glory of winning the World Cup at Wembley in 1966. With their lives ahead of them, money in their pockets and music in their ears, the sixties were fun and exciting times for Jane and Graham. Graham was playing football with his boyhood heroes; Jane danced her way down the aisle, ready to start any adventures that life would throw at the young couple.

After their first date at the pictures in December 1962, chivalrous Graham walked Jane to the bus-stop where she met friend Margaret for the journey home, who'd also had a date that evening. After that, Jane and Graham saw each other regularly. Their buses would arrive in Lichfield Street, Wolverhampton from different directions and they would meet at the entrance to Fleet Electronics (now a sandwich shop) round the corner from the bus stop on Stafford Street, as the entrance would provide some shelter in case of rain. When out dancing with a group of friends, sometimes Graham would miss his bus home, which meant a five mile walk, but via the chippy. As a minor act of teenage rebellion, Graham and his friends would kick the rolled up paper over a factory wall. 'Phil loved telling me that Graham was the only one not to kick the paper over first time,' laughs Jane.

Dating in the sixties meant going to the pictures, and Wolverhampton had a few options: the Gaumont, ABC Savoy and the Odeon. 'There was one called the Clifton but that had sleazy films and was a bit of a flea pit,' says Jane. The Gaumont was also a music venue in the sixties, with both The Beatles and Bill Haley and the Comets playing there. It was destroyed in 1973, with Cliff Richard playing at a farewell concert at the site now covered by Wilko, St George's Parade. The Odeon, on Skinner Street, spent some time as a bingo hall, and is now a Grade Two listed building available to hire as a function room, the Diamond Banqueting Suite. The ill-fated Clifton Cinema is no more. Having started out life as a slaughter house, the cinema closed in 1966, spent some time as a bingo hall before being demolished as it was declared unsafe. The site is now home to the West Midlands Police Station, specialising in screening only crime drama.

Jane took Graham to meet parents Samuel and Muriel in February 1963, and they enjoyed an instant rapport. Brother David would also make a lifelong friend in Graham, although his little sister's new relationship did sometimes require him to make sacrifices. David tells the tale of one occasion during Jane and Graham courtship: 'I'd been working nights and Graham had stayed overnight in my bed as of course they weren't married yet. When I got home at a quarter past seven in the morning my mother's first words were: "You can't go to bed, Graham's in your bed." Graham wasn't his best in the morning and I had to wait until eight thirty when the bed was vacant.'

A few weeks later Graham would take Jane to meet Ernest and Ida, although as Jane discovered many years later, the slight delay in the reciprocal invitation was because Graham, keen to impress, insisted that the living room be painted first. Jane went round for tea and met all the siblings. Little brother Andrew was just a year old and was a big hit. 'I think I fell in love with him instantly, he was such a happy, loving little chap. I think I drove my Mum crazy always talking about Andrew this and Andrew that.' The feeling was mutual it seems, as Andrew laughs: 'I think I might have had a crush on Jane at a very young age LOL, as I would always be sitting next to Jane when she came to our house. They used to go in the back room and I would follow them and Graham would say to Mom: "Can you come and get Andrew - he won't come out the room"!'

Jane's close friends at the time she met Graham were school friends Margaret and Jenny, together with Janet whom she'd befriended on her first day at Queen's Business School. All the girls were working:

Margaret at the GPO, Janet at Sun Life Assurance and Jenny at a solicitors in town. Jane would sometimes meet Jenny in town for lunch at a little cafe on King Street for a fry-up and jam roly-poly pudding. The girls were regular dancing partners and they'd all spend time with Jane and her family, which included accompanying them on their annual summer holiday to Weymouth at the Clifton Hotel ('same hotel, different friend'). Older brother David was off doing his own thing by the time Jane was 14, so younger brother Robert, Jane and a friend would squeeze into the back of Samuel's Ford Zephyr, cases laden on the roof rack. Jane remembers visiting Portland Bill Lighthouse, running up and down the pebbly Chesil Beach and eating fish and chips out of newspaper. Jenny came first in 1960, the following year was Margaret's turn with Janet coming the year after. Jane took her first holiday without her family in 1963, when she went to Butlins Pwlhelli with Janet and family. Jane was in fine company - Queen Elizabeth and her husband Prince Philip paid an official visit to the newly built resort on the ninth of August in the same year. The sweethearts missed each other and wrote to each other; Graham even visited Samuel and Muriel when Jane was away - he was becoming part of the family.

Meanwhile, Graham took his first flight in July 1963 together with the Wolves first team squad, to compete in the Uhrencup at Brühl stadium in Grenchen, Switzerland, an hour north of Bern, as part of pre-season training. The competition was established in 1962, sponsored by the local watch industry (Uhr = watch in German), and is still part of the pre-season circuit - the Wolves squad was back out there in the summer of 2018. Jane was delighted with the watch that Graham brought back as a present for her: 'I wore it for years'. The following year's pre-season training took Graham even further afield, to the Caribbean, playing against Chelsea and local teams in Jamaica, Haiti, Trinidad and Barbados. Jane remembers that Graham had a great time, but was shocked at the poverty in Haiti. Haiti, a former slave colony, gained its independence by defeating their French overlords in the first successful slave rebellion. It remains one of the world's poorest countries and back in the sixties, was ruthlessly governed by Dr Francois Duvalier, known as 'Papa Doc', who had declared himself 'President for Life'. For Graham, the Wolves tours were the start of many overseas adventures: he had caught the travel bug and never looked back.

In October 1963 Graham and Jane went shopping in Wolverhampton and came back with a sparkly engagement ring. Their families were equally delighted and unsurprised. On Christmas Eve their engagement was made official and that evening, the happy couple disappeared off into the sunset on the number 11 bus for an evening of dancing at the Regent with friends. Jane remembers wearing a new black dress from C&A and 'flashing my new ring'.

Graham got his turn for a holiday with the Turners and his now fiancée in 1964, when they went to Southsea together. With less money around, Graham's family holidays had been limited to day trips to Weston-Super-Mare or Blackpool. 'It was a truly wonderful holiday and we had a trip to the Isle-of-Wight on the relatively new hovercraft,' says Jane, 'Graham and I did spend a fair amount of time trying to lose Robert, not always successfully!' The following summer, Graham and Jane took their first holiday as a twosome, staying in a hotel in Margate. All excited about their first romantic dinner together, Jane was harrumphing when the restaurant manager put them on a table with another couple. Making the best of the situation, the foursome got chatting, and found they had an unexpected rapport with their fellow guests, Pauline and Stan. They would go on to become the best of friends and, as is typical of their warm and open nature, Jane and Graham would go on to make many friends on their travels together.

As a Wolves Apprentice, Graham was earning eight pounds a week gross, handed out in a brown paper envelope, and had agreed to give his Mum half of it before realising he'd have to pay tax on it. True to his word, despite this realisation he did give his Mum that four pounds a week, but did have to occasionally ask for subs from his Mum, usually to take out Jane. Things got easier though, as Graham would get a pay rise every year on his birthday. Eldest grand-daughter Lauren realised with delight recently that Grandma was once a WAG, although whilst there was a certain cachet in dating a footballer, they were not big earners. Up until 1961, footballers' wages were capped at £20 a week (compared to an average man's salary of around £14 a week), and the balance of power was firmly tipped in the favour of the employing club rather than the employed player. Jimmy Hill, eighties Match of the Day presenter, former Fulham player and Jimmy Guthrie's successor as chairman of the PFA (Professional Footballers' Association - name changed from the Players' Union to favour an image more akin to actors rather than blue collar workers), threatened strike action and finally the Football League conceded.

Whilst both were earning, and indeed Jane had more disposable income initially, it was the norm for the boys to pay for dates, 'it's just how it was,' and indeed, female financial independence was not rife in the sixties. Despite having manned the factories during the war effort, women's rights in the workplace were few - The Equal Pay Act didn't come about until 1970 after a group of machinists in the Ford factory at Dagenham went out on strike to protest that they were paid less than men doing similar, skilled work. Jane was earning just under five pounds a week at Henry Meadows, and whilst she would put a little aside in savings, she had disposable income to spend on stockings, clothes, make-up and socialising. True Form was Jane's favourite haunt for shoes, C&A a staple for clothes with Richards Dress shop a favourite for special occasions. The night of Jane's first dance with Graham she wore a turquoise blouse, black slim pencil skirt, 'oh, and my three inch heels,' pushing her over the five foot mark. Graham liked to look smart - his 'going-out' outfit would typically be a shirt, tie and slacks, topped off with an M&S sweater. He never actually owned a single pair of jeans.

As well as playing and watching football, Jane and Graham danced their way through the sixties: 'Saturday nights with a group of Graham's friends at the Regent were fantastic,' remembered Jane. She loved dancing, but it wasn't always with Graham or brother David. 'Terry was so good to jive with so we always had a dance together, and Graham with Judi - but years later Graham told me he hated me dancing with Terry.' No doubt he'd said nothing at the time, because he knew how Jane loved to dance and didn't want a little green-eyed moment to spoil the night.

Lots of their friends had coupled up, which meant double dates. Jane's friend Jenny was dating her future husband, Ray, and the four of them spent lots of time together. My husband, Richard, describes Ray as a lovable Del-Boy character, and the first story Jane told me about one time they'd all spent together, certainly fitted the bill. Ray had the benefit of a company car that he was only supposed to use for work, but Ray didn't see any harm in using it to take his friends on a day trip to Blackpool. Jane remembers a great day out, but just outside Stafford, Ray warned them there was a slight problem, that he would have to pull over, that he thought one of the wheels had fallen off. The four friends found a bus back to Wolverhampton, with Ray protesting loudly at the cost of the fare, 'I don't want to buy the bus!' Despite having to explain to his boss on Monday why the car was now three-wheeled and half-way up the M6, Ray was by nature a generous friend, who would use the car to help Graham to learn how to drive. 'We went out lots with Jenny and Ray and we often went back to their flat in Walsall for a beans on toast supper,' said Jane.

It was with Graham's friends Terry and Phil that he and Jane attended one of the many music concerts they would attend together; Jerry Lee Lewis at Bloxwich Baths in March 1964. Now the site of a leisure complex, back then it was a swimming pool, the water covered with boards and transformed into a music venue. 'It was the strangest concert I've ever been to. He just turned up in his mac, took it off and without introducing himself, launched into his repertoire, leg up on the piano belting out 'Great Balls of Fire'. When he'd done, he just put his mac on and left, without a a word,' Jane recalled. At this juncture, it would be remiss of me not to mention that Graham was not Jane's first love, indeed, Graham learned to accept that another man would always be a part of their lives. By nature very loyal, Jane would worship Cliff Richard for a lifetime. First spotted on her black and white TV one Saturday tea-time, on either Juke Box Jury, Oh Boy! or Six-Five Special, popular music shows at the time, it was love at first sight. Jane and friend Jenny first went to see Cliff eight miles away at the Danilo Theatre in Cannock, and Dad Samuel drove the 14 year olds there, coming back to pick them up at the end. After that, the pair never missed Cliff when he came to play in Wolverhampton at the Gaumont (February 1961, February 1962, April 1963 and October 1964!).

Jane hadn't been to a football match before she met Graham, but she would become his most loyal supporter. She first went to watch him play at the training ground at Castlecroft, with its relatively simple facilities, namely a wooden hut that provided little shelter from the elements. Accompanying Jane were two friends from business school, one of whom had a car so they could arrive in style.

Graham's debut with the Wolves first team came when he was 18 years old, in October 1964. His moment came at the end of the Wolves' golden era under Stan Cullis, who had been sacked in September 1964, after 18 years as manager. The Wolves had not started their season well, attendances had fallen below 15,000, but it came as a surprise to many when the club sacked their legendary manager. His replacement, Scotsman Andy Beattie, was not appointed until November 1964. Given the timing of Graham's debut, when the club was between managers, it's not entirely clear who was responsible for giving him his first shot at the big time. However, based on the recollections of Graham's team-mate Terry Wharton in Clive Corbett's book, Those Were the Days, it seems reasonable to assume that Wolves legend and coach at the time, Billy Shorthouse (344 league appearances 1941-1956), might have given Graham the nod. Wharton was clearly not fond of Beattie, describing him as a somewhat absent manager and reported that Shorthouse picked the team as well as delivering training. When I asked Uncle David, who was socialising with many of the players at the time, he concurred: 'Yes, Bill Shorthouse was in charge.'

The game was an away fixture, the Black Country Derby at fierce rivals West Bromwich Albion. Jane went along with brother David. It was a tough start for the central defender, with Wolves losing 5-1. Jeff Astle, who became known as the 'King' by West Brom fans, made his home debut for his new club that day, after being signed from Notts County a few weeks earlier for £25,000. Unfortunately for Graham, it was to be Astle's day as he went on to seal his fate as a firm favourite of the Baggies' fans after putting two of the five goals in the back of the net. Astle would go on to hit the headlines after his untimely death at the age of 59 in 2002. His death was recorded as 'death by industrial injury' - known as an excellent and prolific header of the ball, Astle suffered degenerative brain disease as a result of playing football. Leather balls were used frequently back then, and they became much heavier when wet, and as such were deemed to have caused repeated minor traumas to the brain over the course of his playing career. It was not until the 1986 World Cup when FIFA switched to a fully synthetic ball, having previously used leather balls with a synthetic waterproof coating. Notwithstanding the change in balls, the most recent evidence suggests that football players with long careers, and in particular defenders, are five times more likely to develop dementia than the general population. Five players of England's 1966 World Cup winning team developed dementia. Unaware of this risk when starting out in his career, Graham was lucky to swerve this devastating disease.

A couple of years after his Wolves debut, when interviewed at Preston North End, Graham recalled this match, 'What a nightmare! Jeff Astle and John Kay who scored two goals each, gave us a roasting. The noise from that huge crowd rang in my ears for days.' Jane's brother David recalls Dad Ernie didn't hold back his criticism of Graham as they got back home after the match and put the kettle on: '"Well, you was bloody rubbish," he said, "That was putrid that was." But it wasn't Graham's fault,' says David, 'The back line were past their best. Graham did alright. If Stan Cullis had stayed at Wolves, Graham probably would have stayed and played for the first team. He was certainly good enough.'

Graham didn't like losing, but would never dwell on defeat, knowing that to succeed he had to pick himself up for the next game and continue to fight for his place. After that baptism of fire Graham didn't play first team football again that season, but he continued to be a regular in the reserves, who played their home matches at Molineux in the Central League. The first team continued their downward slide, ultimately getting relegated at the end of the 1964/65 season, but the reserves performed well, finishing towards the top end of their league.

Wolves started their 1965/66 campaign relegated to the second tier of football, for the first time since 1923. Manager Andy Beattie lasted the first nine games of the new season, resigning after a battering from Southampton 9-3 on 18 September. New manager, former England international player Ronnie Allen, gave Graham his next first team outing on 11 December 1965, over a year after his debut. With regular defenders David Woodfield and John Holsgrove injured, Graham was asked to step up. It would be a pattern that would repeat itself throughout Graham's playing time at Wolves; he was not Ronnie Allen's first choice. His Molineux debut, aged 19, was a more successful outing, with Wolves easily overcoming Ipswich 4-1. David was there to watch: 'I can remember Graham and Bobby Thomson hugging at the end of the game.' An auspicious date indeed, birthday of second son Richard some six years later.

Unfortunately Graham was not even considered for Wolves' next match against Middlesbrough the following week due to injury, and whilst he was soon match-fit and playing again for the reserves, he would have to wait several months before his next opportunity to play first team football. That opportunity came when manager Ronnie Allen decided to make some wholesale changes to his team to turn around a run of four games without a win, bringing in Graham and new signing Mike Bailey on 26 March 1966, at home against Norwich. This time, Graham kept his place, becoming a regular first team player until the end of the season. A win at Norwich started a run of six unbeaten games, including a draw against Graham's old boss and Wolverhampton legend, Stan Cullis, manager of local rivals Birmingham City since 1965.

Writing in his column for the Sports Argus, manager Ronnie Allen said of his changes: 'The arrival of Mike Bailey has made a big difference. With he and Ron Flowers we have two really good wing halves. They have been a great help to young Graham Hawkins, who has been introduced at centre-half and made his task of settling in much easier.' Of his new centre half, Ronnie had the following to say: 'A word too about Graham Hawkins, the Darlaston lad who came in at centre-half against Norwich. He had a quiet, confident game and looks like being a useful player. With Ron Flowers and Ken Knighton he made up a half-back line of blondes.' Flowers was club captain and an England international. He would go on that summer to be selected to be part of the 1966 England World Cup squad, although he wouldn't play. Flowers had been a hero of Graham's from his school days of watching Wolves from the South Bank. David remembers seeing Graham play regularly: 'I went to the home games at this time, Graham always had very solid games. But Ron Flowers who looked a lot like Graham and played in front of him was struggling to cover. Graham often had the blame for this.' Aged 31 in March 1966, Flowers was coming to the end of his playing career, and he left Wolves for a player-manager role at Northampton in September 1967, after being unable to play for much of the season due to a back injury. Fast-forward to 2020, grand-daughter and student Holly gets a part-time job through a friend at the Ron Flowers Sports Shop in Wolverhampton, unaware of Flowers' connection to her beloved Grandad. Ken Knighton, Graham's other blonde defensive partner, just a couple of years older than Graham, made 16 league appearances for Wolves before leaving to join Oldham in November 1966, in order to play regular first team football, but it wouldn't be the last time the pair played together.

Wolves' first team finished sixth at the end of that season, not quite doing enough to secure a return to the First Division, but considered strong contenders for promotion the following season. Jane would go and watch home games with Graham's Dad, Ernest, Ida's Dad, Grandad Skitt, with little brother Robert tagging along sometimes. 'Grandad Skitt was a lovely man and Robert was quite envious when he got his sandwich out at half-time, wrapped in the wax paper off a sliced loaf,' remembers Jane. The other players' wives would go too, and Jane became friendly with with wives of Wolves regulars Ron Flowers (Yvonne), David Woodfield (Wendy) and Bobby Thomson (Janice). Post-match entertainment might have involved a trip to the pub. The Kingfisher Country Club in Wall Heath, to the south of Wolverhampton (now gone - Hickory Smokehouse occupied the site in 2019) was a favourite haunt, often featuring live bands, including The Beatles. The club had a swimming pool for added glamour and was the place to be in the sixties.

Graham and Jane enjoyed socialising with the team, their school friends and took in the occasional concert. Jane had her thing for Cliff, whereas Graham and his friends were Bob Dylan fans. In

May 1966, they went as a group to see him at the Birmingham Odeon Theatre (now a cinema, overlooking Birmingham New Street Station). Whilst there were reports of fans turning against Bob Dylan that year, for including an 'electric' set in the second half, Jane and Graham were just happy to see him: 'I soon joined in with their enthusiasm and enjoyed listening to him,' says Jane.

Graham was by now an established player in the Wolves squad, but his experience was very different to that of today's professional footballers. He didn't own a car, and initially, other senior players who lived nearby would pick him up to take him to Molineux, from where the team would take a coach to the training ground. However, after several late arrivals, the coach advised Graham to take the bus and arrive on time, which he duly did. One fan remembers seeing him on the bus back to Bentley, proudly cradling his new boots for the season. Mrs Clamp, mother of senior player, Eddie Clamp, washed the strips and was very much part of the team set-up, 'Mrs Clamp was a strong woman and the players did respect her,' Jane remembers. Half-time refreshments consisted of a cup of tea for both players and fans, with the players treated to oranges as well. Training consisted of playing football and running, lots of running, usually at Cannock Chase just north of Wolverhampton. Graham would train every morning, and often do extra sessions in the afternoon. Many of the senior players would spend the afternoon at the bookies, but that wasn't for Graham. 'He hated losing even two bob so knew big gambling wasn't for him,' said Jane.

'Graham hated pre-season training as they would run and run until most would end up vomiting,' Jane recalled. Sports scientist son Dr Richard Hawkins would go on to be a driver of change in pre-season football training: 'Four to eight minutes of much higher-intensity running are more beneficial than forty minutes of jogging,' he says, although I understand players still vomit after a tough session. Graham disliked running, but knew how important it was to maintain endurance and stuck at it doggedly. During one session, manager Ronnie Allen noticed Graham's discomfort and quipped that he was running like a horse, leading his team-mates to affectionately call him Harry the Horse, a nickname that stuck, ever to be known as Harry

Hawkins, even captured for posterity on vinyl on a record of football songs recorded by the Wolves team in 1967.

The summer of 1966 crowned the England football team champions of the world at Wembley and their success heralded an equally magnificent time for Graham's club as well has his relationship with Jane. The 1966/67 season would see Wolves bounce back, finishing runners-up in the Second Division and thus securing their place in the First Division. Unfortunately Graham found himself unable to secure his slot as first choice, losing out to tough competition for his position. Before the first game of that season, the Sports Argus speculated on Wolves starting 11: 'While Bailey and Flowers are certain starters at half-back, the other position rests between Dave Woodfield, tall John Holsgrove and Graham Hawkins, the Darlaston youngster who created a favourable impression at centre-half in the closing games last season.' The competition for his position meant that Graham found himself frequently playing for the reserves, standing in as 'twelfth man', waiting for his chance when his team-mates were injured. He nonetheless made 27 appearances in that promotion-winning season.

Graham's first appearance in the first team dressing room in that promotion season was as twelfth man in a League Cup game against Mansfield Town, the seventh game of the season on 13 September 1966. Back then, teams were allowed only one substitute and given the risks of going down to ten men or less due to injury, opportunities for the twelfth man to play typically only came when absolutely necessary. Graham was both left and right-footed, and as such would have been a versatile player, well-suited to step in to a number of roles on the pitch. No opportunity came in Wolves' 2-1 win over Mansfield, and Graham's season didn't really get started until four days later when he came on for the injured Holsgrove. Wolves beat Blackburn Rovers comfortably 4-0 and with Flowers injured, Graham played in the following six games, coming off the bench for one of them. His run ended with a 3-1 loss away at Hull City, which came with a consolation of a box of kippers for all of the players, an unexpected 'perk' on the team bus on the way back home. Wolves' performances were mixed and included the highs of a 7-0 win at home against Cardiff, but a stern reminder of the differences between the first and second divisions came with a 5-0 loss against top flight Fulham, ending their hopes of an FA Cup run. Graham came across his old Staffordshire Schools team-mate, Allan Clarke at Craven Cottage that day, with 'Sniffer' getting the better of Graham and scoring two of the five goals. I shared the match report I found on this reunion with twins Derek and David Siveter, and Derek recalled how Alan must have grown since their school days: 'It must have been a bitter-sweet meeting for Graham. Although Sniffer Clarke was the smallest in the South East Staffs side, he lengthened considerably during adolescence and he ended up six feet plus. He was, though, always very skilful with the ball at his feet, a trait that was very obvious when he played for South East Staffs, and presumably one of the main reasons he got picked up by the scouts.'

Graham's next period of regular appearances came in December, when he started in an away win against Norwich after a few games on the bench without playing. The Sports Argus reported that Graham was briefly knocked out during the game, but soon recovered to carry on playing. Now he'd made it onto the pitch off the bench, Graham wasn't going to let a mild concussion take him off it. He kept his place the following game - an away game at Birmingham City where former boss Stan Cullis was also pushing for promotion. On that occasion, it was Birmingham who took the two points for the win, though they ultimately would miss out on promotion. Picked for the first team for the Christmas Eve and Boxing Day matches (a win both at home then away against Derby), it looked like Graham had once again done enough to secure his place in the first team, only to be stretchered off the pitch after 70 minutes on 26th December with torn ankle ligaments thanks to former Leeds United player, Kevin Hector. David remembers the tackle: 'I was at both the Derby games. Kevin Hector and Graham had some history of clashes in the past. The challenge he made to cause injury he would have been sent off in today's games.'

This injury would mean another break of over three months before Graham was back in action for the first team. Whilst he was back in light training by January, and fit by mid-February, he wouldn't get his chance of another run of games until April, with manager Ronnie unwilling to change a winning formula. He managed just 30 seconds of action on 18 March, coming off the bench in the dying seconds for the injured Mike Bailey. This was Graham's first time on the pitch with celebrity signing, Derek Dougan, the 'Doog', who had joined Wolves that month from Leicester for £50,000. Dougan's arrival was well-received by the fans, marked by a hat-trick on his home debut in a 4-0 win against Hull. I suspect the team unanimously preferred the win to a fishy present.

Graham did form part of the starting 11 in the 4-1 win at home against Bury on April 22 1967, a result that secured their promotion to the First Division and the promise of champagne and a bonus to celebrate their achievement. Hungover from winning promotion, Wolves had three games left to secure the top spot in the league, however a loss to ultimate winners, local rivals Coventry City didn't bode well, and despite only needing a draw in their last game, Wolves lost away at Crystal Palace, gifting the title to Coventry City. The award for 'Tomorrow's Top Manager' duly went to Jimmy Hill, Coventry City's manager, with Ronnie Allen as runner-up.

In May 1967, the club hosted a civic reception in the Town Hall, celebrating the team's promotion. Jane remembers wearing an orange halter-neck dress from C&A and all the players and wives receiving a gift of a fob watch on a chain. The term 'WAG' was yet to be coined, but the summer of 1967 certainly brought some of the glamour to Wolverhampton. Jane remembers meeting Jutta, Dougan's glamorous wife, who knew how to dress to impress. Dougan sadly died suddenly of a heart attack in 2007, and in one of the biographies written in the aftermath (The Doog: The Incredible Story of Derek Dougan by David Harrison and Steve Gordos), Jutta described her experiences of watching from the stands in that promotion-winning season: 'At Wolves' home games the players' wives would sit on the first row. It was a fashion show and one could not go to matches in the same outfit twice. Sometimes the season ticket holders behind us would give out abuse to the team. If one of the wives said, "How dare you call my husband that?", they would reply, "Shut up. At least we paid for our tickets, unlike you".'

A MARRIAGE MADE IN FOOTBALL

Wedding planning was well underway when the call came for Graham to join the Wolves team in Los Angeles, playing in a competition including European and South American teams, organised and funded by a group of American and Canadian entrepreneurs. The competition was designed to launch a US professional league in a land yet to show much interest in 'soccer'. The Wolves competed as 'LA Wolves' in the Western Division, alongside five other teams, the final to be played against the winners of the Eastern Division. The tour was six weeks long, but clashed with Graham and Jane's wedding date. Jane has some regrets: 'At the time, I couldn't imagine changing the date, but over the years thought we should have, as LA Wolves went on to win.' Graham flew out to LA with the team, but was given permission to return after three weeks to get married. It was a glamorous trip by all accounts, involving socialising with Davy Jones of the Monkees and the Four Tops in the clubs of Los Angeles, as well as plenty of success on the football, or rather 'soccer', field.

Graham shared a room with Dougan on that US trip - in an interview with David Harrison of the Wolverhampton Express and Star, he laughed: 'I think I was the only player who was prepared to put up with all of his talking.' Dougan was eight years Graham's senior, an experienced player who in 1967 applied unsuccessfully for the post of chairman of the PFA (he would go on to serve as chairman from 1970 - 1978), whereas Graham's professional career was just beginning, but there must have been a positive connection between the pair. Graham went on to leave Wolves just nine months after Dougan arrived, oblivious of the role that the dynamic Irishman would go on to play in his life some 15 years' later.

Jane and Graham wed on 26 June 1967, both aged 21, at the Holy Trinity Church, Heath Town. Ray was best man, and as a 'good talker' gave a great speech. Graham's younger sister Susan was a bridesmaid, then aged 13, together with Jane's friends Jenny and Margaret. Jane had served as Jenny's bridesmaid the year before and would repeat the favour for Margaret and her husband, Alan, the following year. Graham's team-mates couldn't make it, given they were still playing football in America, but their wives came, keen for updates from Graham on what their husbands were up to. It was a fabulous day, starting at 11am in the church, finishing for most with chicken, white wine and Asti Spumante in the Connaught Hotel, Tettenhall Road, but little brother Robert, a little tipsy and full of food, found himself back at school in the afternoon sitting his maths 'O' level (he passed). As was tradition, wedding gifts were not extravagant but designed to help the young couple to set up home. Graham's pals and team-mates Mike Bailey and Ernie Hunt teamed up to co-ordinate their gifts, one buying the iron, the other the ironing board.

Jane and Graham drove to Bristol for their wedding night before going on to Newquay in Cornwall for a week's honeymoon. Graham had passed his driving test that February, and on the advice of a friend, bought his first car, an Austin A40, 'it got us on honeymoon and back home - then the bottom fell out,' reported Jane. Thankfully they got a few more miles out of their next car, a Ford Anglia.

Jane and Graham started married life in their first home together, a three-bed semi-detached house in 19, Ravenhill Drive, Codsall, just outside Wolverhampton, with a mortgage provided by Wolves. 'I loved everything about our first home. Mum helped with lots of cooking advice, my Dad delivered our coal - free of charge of course. Graham drove me to work at Meadows and we listened to Tony Blackburn on the car radio - Radio One was brand new. I would wait at Mum and Dad's for Graham to pick me up after work,' said Jane. Graham received a £500 bonus in recognition of his five years at Wolverhampton Wanderers, and used this money to buy furniture to set up home. In the days before IKEA, furniture was relatively expensive - average weekly earnings in 1967 were approximately £14 (c. £700p.a.). Jane still has the dressing table bought for £45, which, if using today's average annual earnings would equate to around £1,700. Built to last.

The start of the 1967/8 football season soon came around, and whilst Jane was setting up their new home together as a married couple, it was business as usual for Graham. He had to sit out the first part of the season though, making a few appearances on the bench, but not breaking through into the starting 11. On 4th November 1967, during a home game against fellow promotees, Coventry City, Graham was sent on by Ronnie Allen for the injured Dave Wagstaffe ('Waggy') just before half-time, only to be shoved off the pitch by Derek Dougan. Dougan, well-known for being fearless in expressing his opinions of how things should be done, seemed to be making the executive decision to see if Waggy would come around during half-time. No doubt manager Allen had a few choice words for Dougan, and Graham duly made his way out to start the second half. Wolves won 2-0. Jane remembers quietly seething sitting in a row with the rest of the players' wives and girlfriends, including Dougan's wife Jutta.

Graham was enjoying his football at Wolves, but was keen to make more first team appearances. Graham just wasn't Allen's kind of player, and his playing career could have been very different, had Stan Cullis remained in charge. Ronnie Allen, a well-respected manager, had a different vision for Wolves and had brought in John Holsgrove and Mike Bailey, both of whom were selected ahead of Graham when fit. An opportunity for more regular first team football would come at the close of 1967, when Preston North End made an offer. Allen told Graham of the approach and having discussed it with Jane, the newly-weds decided they were up for an adventure up the newly-built M6. Before the days of powerful football agents, Graham managed negotiations himself and three trips to Preston later, the deal was done and he'd earned himself 10% of the £35,000 transfer fee. Ray drove up on the third visit as it was a Saturday, and after the deal was done, they all went into Preston for some lunch, with Ray commenting: 'Can't believe I've just driven my mate to sign for another club and move away.'

Graham played his last game at Molineux on 30 December 1967, losing 3-2 to visitors Manchester United, with England legend Bobby Charlton opening the scoring. Whilst losing to Manchester United must have hurt at the time, playing against the team containing George Best, considered by many to be the best team in the world, was a fantastic achievement. Graham had to pick himself up from many disappointments in the early years of his football career and fight for his place in the Wolves team, showing resilience that can mean the difference between success and failure in a highly competitive environment. He'd been a popular member of the team - team-mates Ernie Hunt and Mike Bailey both wrote about their pal 'Harry Hawkins' in their weekly columns with great fondness. On Graham's penultimate game, at Old Trafford against Manchester United, Mike Bailey joked about Graham's pre-match ritual - sitting motionless in the dressing room before jumping up with a 'That's It!' at exactly two thirty, getting changed ready for the three o'clock kick off. With luck playing a role in many football matches, footballers can be a superstitious lot. Superstitions aside, with Jane by his side, Graham was nevertheless ready for a new adventure up north.

A MARRIAGE MADE IN FOOTBALL

Jane and Graham with baby Richard and toddler Ian, 1972.

3 Bye Bye Black Country, Hello Lilywhites

1968 – 1974 Lytham Part One

Preston North End, like Wolverhampton Wanderers, is a club steeped in history and one of the 12 founder members of the English Football League in 1888, the oldest such institution of professional football teams in the world. The founding of the League represented the beginnings of football as England's national sport, and a sport played for and by the working classes. Graham and Jane's move to Lancashire kept them close to the heart of the roots of football.

Wolves had enjoyed a golden period of success under Stan Cullis, whose sacking coincided with the start of Graham's first team debut in 1964. Similarly, Preston's golden era was tied to the career of one man, namely Sir Tom Finney. During the 14 years Finney was in charge as manager, other than two seasons in Division Two, Preston were secure in the First Division. After Finney retired in 1960, the club lost direction and was beset with financial difficulties fought off with regular fire-sales of their star players. When Graham arrived at the beginning of 1968, Preston were in (old money) Division Two and would never return to the top flight. Nevertheless, Graham got the regular first team football he was looking for and would go on to make 269 appearances for Preston North End (compared to 35 at Wolves). During Graham's time at Preston North End he became a father, a captain and a role model to thousands of football fans.

One such fan is Edward Skingsley, a lifelong Preston North End fan who had religiously followed his team and was inspired to write a book, A Season to Savour, documenting match by match the

1970/1971 season using notes he'd made on programmes and newspaper cuttings he'd saved since he was a child. After getting the writing bug, Skingsley went on to write and publish two further books on Preston North End covering The Sixties and The Seventies as well as contributing 'Memory Lane' pieces on Preston North End for the Lancashire Evening Post. Graham met with Skingsley in 2015 and subsequently agreed to write the foreword to A Season to Savour. The two men ended up spending many hours together sharing football stories, connecting over their mutual love and appreciation of Preston North End. Skingsley's books have been invaluable in giving me insight into Graham's footballing time at Preston North End, not least because sadly many of Graham's fellow players are no longer with us. When I asked Skingsley about that meeting, his response was deeply felt:

> 'I had contacted Graham a year or two earlier to ask if he wanted some DVDs I had of Preston North End while he was there. He was very nice with me considering I had called him out of the blue, and said of course he would, and I actually seem to recall him saying, "these will be great for my granddaughters to see what I got up to…" I felt ten feet tall after the conversation ended. Here was my boyhood hero, the rock of the North End defence, always around 30 yards away from me, talking to me as he would anybody else. I couldn't wait to tell anyone who would listen. With trepidation I contacted him again about the foreword. It was all positive, and in the course of the conversation Graham suggested a meeting at a pub just off the M6 "for an hour". I was so, so grateful to him; he was so engaging and helpful, he was what every kid would want his hero to be. The conversation went on for ages, well past the hour expected. "Graham we've been yakking away for nearly two hours, do you have to get away?", "No, I'm enjoying this!". We carried on. He had done such a lot in the game and his life and achieved plenty.'

In summing up, Skingsley describes his meeting with Graham as 'an afternoon of complete and utter awe for me.' Graham's pleasure in the encounter is evident in his foreword to Skingsley's book, which he concludes by saying: 'Having read a sneak preview of the book, I am sure you are going to enjoy it. It paints a very good picture from a supporter's point of view, bringing in all the tension and excitement of that great season.'

The DVDs gifted to Graham by Skingsley found their way into my hands via Jane, and so I got to watch several hours of Graham playing football from the late sixties to the mid-seventies. I saw the hair and side-burns grow to epic proportions, brutal tackles barely acknowledged by referees and pitches my son's U14 coach would consider unplayable. Graham is a blonde Adonis, muscular and fearless. A confident, vocal captain whom the commentators describe frequently using 'solid', 'dependable' and 'keeping his head'. In the local derby away against Blackpool in April 1973, towards the end of a difficult season in which they would ultimately be relegated from Division Two, striker Hugh McIlmoyle is interviewed after the match and asked his feelings about the stalwart Hawkins. Five minutes into that match Preston goalkeeper Alan Kelly had been concussed and stretchered off, and with only one substitute, McIlmoyle pulled on the green shirt (amazingly no gloves) and took Kelly's place admirably. McIlmoyle confirmed that Hawkins was a great motivator of the side, a great leader and most noticeably so when things were difficult for the team, 'especially now we're struggling, he's real lion-hearted you know'. He also won most of his headers, picked out players with pin-point accuracy and although I wouldn't say he ran like a horse, he worked like one.

Skingsley also told me that Graham had given him his collection of football programmes, knowing how much he would treasure it. Jane had been looking for them when I started asking her difficult questions about Graham's playing career: 'I wondered what had happened to them!' she laughed.

Whilst Jane and Graham were only relocating a couple of hundred miles away from Wolverhampton, moving away from family was nonetheless atypical for the average working class couple in the sixties, in an era before foreign travel became the norm. Where Wolverhampton was the heart of the black country, Preston was steeped in the cotton mills of the industrial revolution, pressed into the white shirts of the football team giving them the nickname, the

'Lilywhites'. Their move in January 1968, meant Jane and Graham would only get to spend a few months in their new house. They didn't have to worry about selling the Codsall house as Wolverhampton Wanderers FC were happy to take it off their hands to use as a club house for new players. Wolves' new signing Derek Parkin was next in the house, at the time the most expensive full-back in England when he signed for £80,000, and would go on to make 609 first team appearances. Footballers may not have been paid the eye-watering salaries received nowadays, but many clubs did try and act as surrogate parents for their young players. Like ships in the night once more, Derek Parkin would go on to leave struggling Wolves in 1982 for Stoke City, shortly before Graham's appointment as manager.

Their second home together was be a new-build house - a three-bedroomed dormer bungalow on Tewkesbury Drive in Lytham. Jane described the move: 'Ken Knighton, who had been at Wolves then Oldham, was signed by Preston in the same season and had already chosen a house on the estate in Lytham and we put our names down for the adjoining semi…I loved this house - being as it wasn't complete we were able to pick colours and have a York stone fireplace built. It was light and airy, there was a field at the back, lovely views and we were able to walk to Lytham Green and the shops.' Fellow players Archie Gemmill (Preston 1967-1970 after which he went on to great success under Brian Clough at First Division Derby) and Clive Clark (joined Preston in 1970) also lived on the same new estate, as did Bobby Seith (Preston manager 1968 - 1970). Their new house wouldn't be ready until May, so the first few months of 1968 involved a fair bit of travel up and down the M6. Jane would travel up and watch home games, Graham would stay on his own in a guesthouse after away games. Auntie Dot, mother Muriel's sister, came to keep Jane company in Wolverhampton when she was left on her own for the first time.

Graham signed on the dotted line for Preston North End under manager Jimmy Milne on 13 January 1968, and made his first appearance two weeks later at a cup game against Queens Park Rangers in London. It wasn't a very auspicious start, with Graham coming off injured after just five minutes. He'd not been playing regular first team football for Wolves, but had featured regularly as

12th man - missing out on game time as he wouldn't have played in the reserves, possibly increasing his risk of injury. In later years, Richard would often discuss with his Dad how muscle injuries can be prevented with the right preparation, leaving Graham to rue how that knowledge could have helped him in his playing days.

Come March 1968, the furniture was put into storage and the newly-weds took up residence in a B&B near the Preston stadium at Deepdale for a few weeks whilst they waited for their house to be finished. Whilst Graham was training in the mornings, Jane remembers a sturdy, slightly mystical Polish landlady who took her under her somewhat intimidating wing. With Graham injured, the pair got back to visit family back in Wolverhampton, and former Wolves team-mate Mike Bailey mentions a visit from Graham in his weekly column at the end of April 1968: 'Two of our old pals and former clubmates, Fred Davies[1] and Graham Hawkins popped in to see us this week. Both are doing well for their respective clubs, Cardiff City and Preston. 'Harry' Hawkins has now completely recovered from the injury he met with shortly after joining Preston and is now back in the first team at centre-half. Playing alongside him is Ken Knighton, another ex-Molineux favourite. Harry is confident now that Preston who have spent substantially in recent months to strengthen their team, will be able to stay up.' Manager Milne was impressed with Graham, and asked him to be team captain, recognising his leadership qualities at the relatively young age of 21, but Graham showed considerable self-awareness in soon relinquishing the armband as he felt the responsibility was too soon, preferring to focus on his football and settle into his new club. He talked about the decision to hand back the armband in an interview that was featured in a subsequent match program: 'Previously I was inclined to doubt myself. Also, I perhaps tried to take on too much in view of my limited experience - the captaincy for instance…I found it did not help me at all. I had a job to do and might have done it better but for worrying, as captain, over what the other fellows were doing. My confidence suffered.'

Graham and Jane's new house was ready the day before The FA Cup Final in May 1968, as was Graham, coming out of hospital after having his tonsils removed. Jane had got on the bus from the

B&B to visit Graham shortly after the operation, and was very upset to find that he couldn't speak. Later that day she rang her Mum on the payphone, worried he'd never speak again. Thankfully, her fears proved unfounded, and the TV was set up just in time for kick-off on 20 May 1968, so they could watch the same Jeff Astle who'd run rampant on Graham's Wolves debut, win the cup for West Brom with an extra-time goal against Everton. Well-known for shouting at footballers on the TV, it was probably one of Graham's quieter football games.

Despite the couple moving so far away from family, everyone was happy for them, rallying round to help out when needed. Jane said: 'The families didn't mind us moving away, they knew it was going to happen at some point, just not so quickly. They really made it easy for us and we used to try and get back to see everyone every five or six weeks….Jenny and Ray visited us loads of times, David also visited lots and used to go to the games too. Graham's family loved to visit and also my Mum and Dad and a variety of friends. Bob[2] and Diane came too when they started courting as did David and Angela. Maureen used to come up on the train and stay a few days.' Friends Jenny and Ray would start to refer to Jane and Graham as 'our friends on the coast'.

As well as maintaining their friendships back in Wolverhampton, Jane and Graham quickly made new friends and started their social life in Lancashire. Jane got a secretarial job at Sunblest bakery and Graham easily settled into life at Preston North End, as did Jane. She recalls: 'The club was so much smaller than Wolves but very friendly and made you very welcome. It was a good close friendly squad. It was different in as much as at Wolves, Graham had been part of the club for six years and at Deepdale he went in the team as an exciting addition who would bolster their defence.' Back in 1968 and indeed until 1981, teams received just two points for a win and one for a draw, which meant football was arguably more defensive than it is today; teams today are more likely to fight on for a win and the considerably greater prize of three points. Graham's defensive qualities would indeed be appreciated by his new club.

BYE BYE BLACK COUNTRY, HELLO LILYWHITES

Lytham was altogether more sedate than nearby Blackpool and Preston - nights out there would be in one of its cozy pubs, including the Ship and Royal which is still open today. With the seventies on the horizon, disco was replacing the old dance halls - dancing was at either The Lemon Tree, a club on the South Shore in Blackpool (long gone) as well as the Piper in Preston, a favourite of the players on a Saturday night after the game. The Piper was in a single storey building, opposite the bus station on Tithebarn Street in central Preston. Jane and Graham became good friends with the owner of the Piper, Leno. Jane's brother David also became a big fan of the Piper, although some of the players' wives were known to complain to Jane that David was a bad influence on them. David remembers fun times in Preston, and was a frequent visitor, and who's to say if he was a bad influence or not, but he does have a few tales of 'scrapes'. One such tale came about in a Lytham pub when sixties crooner Englebert Humperdinck demanded David and Graham give up one of their bar stools with the immortal line: 'Do you know who I am?' Piqued, David was rolling his sleeves up when 'gentle giant' Graham stepped in to smooth things over. 'I used to box you see, and so I couldn't officially hit anyone,' David laughs. Humperdinck aside, David will typically happily chat to anyone, celebrity or no, and recalls a long chat with Oscar-winning actor Albert Finney who was at the golf club with Sean Connery one time he was enjoying a round with Graham. Lytham has a famous golf course, frequented by many celebrities to this day, and in the sixties and seventies, entertainers would often take in a round when up to perform in Blackpool.

It was during the Preston years, that Graham met Bob Rhodes, Preston fan and former professional boxer who serviced many of the Preston North End players' cars at his garage in Preston. Graham and he became good friends, and then business partners. Together with next-door-neighbour and fellow Preston player, Ken Knighton, Graham invested in Bob's business, the Kent St Garage. Training over, Graham would head over to the garage to help out with the books as well as learn a thing or two about fixing cars. When Bob got divorced, he moved into a little flat above the garage and Richard remembers visiting with brother Ian and Mum Jane and being shocked by the pictures of naked ladies on the walls. (The Sun newspaper had launched its controversial 'page three' featuring topless models in 1970 and doubled its circulation in the process.) Jane would make sandwiches for Bob that Graham would take over on his way to training, and Bob would babysit for Ian and Richard when they had a football 'do' to attend. Jane's 'boy racer' brother David got his first sports car through the garage - an orange MG BGT.

Although they didn't know it at the time, that summer of 1968 would be the last before taking on the responsibilities of impending parenthood. Graham and Jane took their first overseas holiday together, to Ibiza with friends Jenny and Ray, the first time on a plane for three out of four of them: 'a brilliant holiday, never stopped laughing', remembers Jane. The Fawlty Towers elements of their holiday, ants in the rooms, unfinished hotel and the same tinned peaches for dessert every evening, didn't detract from their fun. It proved to be an eventful trip in many ways - Ray even saved a young boy from drowning in the hotel pool - the boys' friends had thought he was just larking about.

Preston had hung on to their spot in Division Two at the end of the season in 1968, finishing a lowly 20th, but the new season saw the manager who had signed Graham, Jimmy Milne, move 'upstairs' to join the board and new manager and neighbour, Scotsman Bobby Seith take his first managerial post. Seith was well-liked and respected by the players, a 'decent chap'. Graham, apart from a few injury-enforced absences, was a regular first team player in his first full season at Preston and had notched up 42 appearances. In 1969, the team finished a more respectable 14th, clear of relegation, but not yet challenging for promotion to the top tier. Jane went to all of the first team games with the other players' wives and whoever was visiting at the time, and enjoyed a much-appreciated cup of tea and a scone or cake at half-time when at home at Deepdale. Slightly less appreciated by Jane, was the Miss Preston North End competition: 'The time Graham was captain, he presented the winner with sash and cup and a kiss. He knew I hated it and he just laughed.' Photographs from the time attest to what a striking couple Graham and Jane were and there were moments where they had to fend off unwanted attention. Jane got a phone call one day from the barber where she would take Ian and Richard for their haircuts, the same one used by Graham and many of the Preston players, asking her to join him for a coffee. Assuming it was an innocent invitation, it was only when he started suggesting they find somewhere to go where she wouldn't know anyone, that she twigged that he was making moves. The amorous hairdresser might have lived to regret his brazen approach, when later that day he got an abrupt call from Graham informing him that the family and players would no longer be frequenting his establishment.

Jane and Graham enjoyed their first couple of years of married life with no pressures, and various sightseeing trips. When not playing matches, Graham would train every morning, but always keen to use his time to good effect, would do extra running in the afternoons and through his friendship with Leno from the Piper Club, started coaching the Piper football team. 'They would train one night a week with Graham and play Sunday morning....They were a great bunch of lads and we had some super end of season presentation dances,' Jane recalled, 'One Sunday one of the players turned up in a dress suit, he came straight from a night out.' Many professional players struggled with the lure of the snooker hall and the bookies in the afternoons and Graham was determined that wasn't a trap he was going to fall into. Graham got the first taste of success as manager of the Piper team - four times league champions, three times cup winners - yes it was non-league football, but he was learning he had the attributes of a football manager.

In March 1969 Jane fell pregnant with Ian. Their doctor advised Jane to put her feet up, concerned there was a risk of miscarriage, and as was usual back then, she immediately left her job. Women were routinely sacked for getting pregnant until the late seventies - maternity pay and rights were first introduced in the Employment Protection Act in 1975. Graham was earning enough for this not to be a worry for them and Jane has fond memories: 'it was a really lovely time being pregnant in 1969 - I went to ante-natal classes at the Lytham Cottage Hospital where I also saw my doctors, who had loads of time to talk about anything that was bothering you.' The Lytham Cottage Hospital was housed in a beautiful old building dating from 1871, just under a mile from Tewksbury Drive, but was sadly demolished in 2007. The ante-natal classes gave Jane advice on what foods to eat whilst pregnant, breathing techniques for labour and she remembers bathing a plastic doll and relaxing at the end with a bit of a lie down on a mat, when usually one of the women would fall asleep.

Jane did suffer a little from morning sickness in the early stages of her pregnancy, but that wasn't going to stop their planned trip to The FA Cup Final at Wembley on 20 April 1969, where she and Graham, team-mate Ken Knighton and wife Carol together with 100,000 fans watched Manchester City beat Leicester City by a single goal in the 24th minute.

The summer of 1969 took Graham away again - this time he'd been selected, together with Knighton to go on a tour of the Far East and New Zealand as part of a 17-man FA squad (England 'A' team) led by Jimmy Armfield, a lifelong Blackpool player and captain for ten years (1954-71, predominantly in the top flight) and member of the 1966 England World Cup-winning squad. The team played five matches between 21st May and 2nd June 1969, winning them all comfortably, including an 11-0 win. The trip was an amazing experience, taking in Hong Kong (where Graham bought his cine camera), Bangkok, Kuala Lumpur, Tahiti and New Zealand. Both modest and insightful, Graham talked about the experience in one Preston North End interview, 'I was rather lucky to get in, due to Alan Bloor[3] not being able to make the trip. But I would not have missed the opportunity for anything. I picked up a bit of what every player needs, namely confidence…Previously I was inclined to doubt myself.'

When Graham wasn't around, Jane would get the bus or other players would help out with lifts, but with a baby on the way and Graham away at the other side of the world, Jane decided that the time had come to learn to drive. Like Graham, she passed first time, but with a rather large bump at six months pregnant. Graham was often away, but Jane was happy to keep busy, spending time back in Wolverhampton with family or entertaining friends and family at home. Jane also enjoyed spending time with other players' wives when the boys were away, Carol Knighton, Ken's wife, was just next door and Pat Ross, wife of player George Ross, also became a good friend.

BYE BYE BLACK COUNTRY, HELLO LILYWHITES

Preston North End's season hadn't got off to a great start in 1969, with the fans registering their dissatisfaction by singing (to the tune of John Lennon's Give Peace a Chance) 'All we are saying, is give us a goal', but the imminent arrival of Baby Hawkins was a welcome distraction. The baby was due on 28th December, but Graham was due to be away training all day and so Jane went into hospital the evening before, even though not in labour. In the early hours of the due date contractions began and Baby Ian arrived at 6.35am. 'It was a foggy morning,' said Jane, 'and when I got no reply from my call I started to worry, rang Ken (Knighton) and Carol next door and they went to wake him up.' As was usual back then, Jane spent the following ten days in hospital, so over the new year, but she remembers a fun time, 'the nurses were brilliant and they were having a party upstairs and brought down treats for us, and to check on us.'

Jane's mother Muriel came up to Lytham to visit to meet her first grandchild, and baby Ian went on his first trip to Wolverhampton at around four weeks old to meet Graham's family. Then Auntie Dot came to stay. Jane did appreciate Dot's help in the early days with baby Ian, particularly as he seemed to be a baby who didn't want much sleep. After six weeks, however, Graham and Jane were ready to send Dot back to Wolverhampton, and enjoy their time together with their new baby. Conscious that in order to perform on the pitch, Graham needed his sleep, Jane would spend many hours out pram-pushing along the sea front at Lytham with friends, as well as partaking in 'lots of tea and cakes.' Richard tells me that one of his earliest memories is of his Mum telling him and Ian to be quiet, as Dad 'needed his sleep'.

Jane's mother, Muriel came to visit again in Easter 1970, leaving Dad, Samuel at home with Jane's brothers, David and Robert, now 26 and 20. Big brother David was by now working with Samuel in the coal delivery business and younger brother Robert was at Aston University in Birmingham, studying metallurgy on a sandwich course whilst also working. Samuel rang one evening to let Muriel know that he'd sold both of the houses on Cannock Road having received an unexpected offer. A developer bought seven or so adjacent houses and the land was developed into a petrol station (now home to Enterprise Rent-A-Car). Brother Robert had painted 'WW' in big white letters on the back garden wall, that survived for many years on what became the wall of the petrol station. Muriel soon forgave Samuel for his impulsiveness, when she discovered that a house she'd admired for many years was up for sale, and Lindum, Victoria Road, just a five minute walk from Cannock Road, became their new home. In April 1970 Jane got her first viewing of her parents' new house on the occasion of Ian's christening, when a merry band of friends and family, including new godparents Jenny and Ray, trooped back for refreshments after the ceremony at the Holy Trinity Church, where Graham and Jane got married.

1970 proved to be a difficult year for English football as well as Preston North End - after bringing home the World Cup four years earlier, the England football team lost to Germany in the quarter finals in Mexico. The Lilywhites finished 22nd in Division Two and were duly relegated. Seith and his coach, Bryan Edwards, were sacked after the penultimate match - a further blow for the players, who both liked and respected their manager. Skingsley reported that 'for the remaining match, a couple of nominated senior players would assist chairman Tom Nicholson with team selection while ex-full back Willie Cunningham put his hand up, volunteering to be temporary trainer.' It was hard being relegated, but Jane was stoic - 'you just got on with it' - glorious victories and crushing defeats were all part of football. Around Lytham, most were fans of local rivals, Blackpool, and so Graham was not really bothered by any local disgruntled supporters. Living in the heart of your team's fans is something to be avoided for footballers, to allow for some sanctuary when the inevitable poor run of form happens. For the England football team, the poor run of form would last for several years longer, failing to qualify for the World Cup in both 1974 and 1978.

A number of players put in transfer requests, including Graham, but the board asked him to reconsider, and he would go on to play a pivotal role in the 1970/71 season, providing the inspiration and material to schoolboy Skingsley for the book he would write decades later. The summer of 1970 saw the arrival of Alan Ball Senior, father to Alan Ball Junior, 1966 World Cup Winner, as Preston's new manager and the mood soon changed. Blunt and a hard task master,

BYE BYE BLACK COUNTRY, HELLO LILYWHITES

'Bally' made his presence felt immediately. 'Alan Ball welcomed us that season by not even showing us a football for a couple of weeks - it was run, run and run some more,' Graham explained in the foreword to Skingsley's book. Joining Ball as assistant, was Arthur Cox, an experienced coach who went on manage Newcastle United in the First Division for four years in the eighties, meeting Graham on the touchline as his opponent at Wolves. Graham described the style of the two men to Skingsley: 'Arthur Cox was Bally's right hand man, and their preparation for games was meticulous. We knew what the opposition would try to do but more importantly we knew what we had to do. We also had to know and understand our team-mates' jobs too - not just our own. Those Friday morning pre-match meetings were so long they would sometimes see Bally get through a full packet of 20 cigarettes!'

A pre-season tour took Preston to Scotland and again, Graham was asked to be team captain, but this time he was ready to accept. Skingsley had this to say: 'It must have been easy for Ball to nominate Hawkins as captain. He had it all. Blessed with commanding presence and a reading of the game that isn't conferred on many, he led by example throughout the season. Never taking a backward step, he organised and protected. Not short of all round ability either, often supplementing the attack with his aerial skills. Ever present. Colossus.'

Not many Preston fans would have predicted that their team would finish league champions in 1971, especially after star player Archie Gemmill was persuaded to move to Derby by Brian Clough (this moment is dramatised in the 2014 film about Clough starring Michael Sheen, That Damned United) for £70,000. (Derby, with Gemmill, would go on to be First Division Champions in 1972). Ball had a clear strategic vision and knew how to motivate his players, and would end up winning the league without any big ticket signings. Bobby Ham arrived from Bradford for £8,000 in October and then went on to score on his debut, but Ball's attempts to sign Kevin Keegan from Scunthorpe came to nought, with Liverpool ultimately scooping the talented 20 year old for just £30,000.

A MARRIAGE MADE IN FOOTBALL

Ball was full of praise for his captain, Graham, with this to say about him after a clean sheet earned an important away point at Bristol: 'My centre half and skipper, Graham Hawkins was superb and must be worth £150,000, while John Bird who I signed a few weeks ago for only £5,000 is already worth £20,000.'

The penultimate game of the season was away against the league leaders, Fulham and the crunch game was captured on film. A goal from Ricky Heppolette, their Indian-born striker, secured the win and promotion. The team were pumped up for the final game of the season against Rotherham United - their 3-0 win secured the title - Graham reported: 'We were prepared very well by Bally for that final game against Rotherham United and there was no way we were not lifting that title!' Great celebrations followed, with Preston honouring the team in their tens of thousands in front of the beautiful Harris Library. 'I was very proud to be North End captain at that special time, and that pride stays with me even today,' Graham told Skingsley in 2015.

After a short break from football in June, July 1971 saw Graham go off once more on pre-season training with Preston. Football life means that the summer holidays and Christmas are not typical family times, which along with frequent trips away, can put pressure on a relationship. Jane is typically sanguine about it, knowing that was what she signed up for. She married Graham fully briefed on what a life in football could bring and was happy to accept the ups and the downs that came with the game. Come what may, she trusted in Graham's judgment and talent. For Graham, whilst pre-season was about getting physically ready for the endurance challenge ahead, it was also a time for team-bonding and some fun before the pressures of performing week after week kicked in. There was less attention paid by the press to pre-season matches, it was a time for coaches to experiment, and to that effect, Graham would sometimes play as a forward. Furthermore, football clubs didn't have the funds for large squads, so players needed to be flexible. In one pre-season game against Dutch team Groningen on 4th August 1971, however, local paper the Lancashire Evening News found a newsworthy story when Graham managed to miss three penalties. The referee ordered re-takes as the goalkeeper kept coming off his line before the shot was taken, but having saved the third, despite the goalkeeper re-offending, the referee gave up and ordered the teams to play on. The evening paper reported Graham's misfortune with the headline, 'Try try, try again….but you don't always succeed - just ask Graham Hawkins!' Ed Skingsley kindly dug out the article from the Lancashire Archives for me, in which journalist Norman Shakeshaft gamely debates whether or not Graham's efforts were in fact worthy of a world record: 'A record? Well, when such a long-established authority on football as former Post sports editor, Walter Pilkington, says that he cannot recall a similar thing happening in his many years of soccer reporting, I think it must be.' Record or not, it was a story Graham happily shared, recognising the funny side.

In early 1971, Jane and Graham were ready to have more children, thinking that a two year age gap would be nice, and sure enough, planned to perfection, Jane was pregnant again with baby number two due on Christmas Eve. Jenny and Ray had come to stay, bringing Christmas presents from family in Wolverhampton, but Richard did not want to wait and in the early hours of 11 December 1971 he let everyone know he was on his way. Graham's car was blocked in by Ray's, so their friends were unexpectedly woken for car shuffling, so Graham could take Jane to the hospital. Graham went off to play that Saturday afternoon against second-placed Millwall, helping them on to a glorious 4-0 win.

With two young boys in tow, Jane didn't go out so much in the early seventies, but there were regular Saturday nights out for Graham and the team after a game, often in the Piper Club in Preston. 'People used to ask me if it bothered me,' said Jane, 'but of course it didn't. It was part of football.' Graham didn't really drink to excess, but there was the odd occasion when it got the better of him - Jane remembers him being ill after a night out on Christmas Eve 1971, no doubt 'wetting' baby Richard's head. Despite emptying the contents of his stomach on his return home, he still managed to build Ian's rocking horse in time for Christmas Day. Uncle David chuckles as he remembers a night out in Lytham when 'Graham tried to take on

Angela[4] by matching her Bacardi and Cokes and lost, spending the night with his head over a toilet bowl.'

The 1971/72 season saw Preston finish 18th in the Second Division, surviving but without cause for any major celebrations. The highlight was a fourth round FA Cup tie against Manchester United, featuring the mighty strike force of George Best, Denis Law and Bobby Charlton. Unfortunately Graham was injured and didn't play in the match, but the team hung on for 85 minutes before succumbing to two late goals to take them out of the competition. After the match, manager Ball was bullish in support of his players and disappointed not to get a replay over in Manchester: 'If we had gone to Old Trafford with Graham Hawkins back in the centre of defence and Neil Young in the attack, we would have been looking for more than just a percentage of the gate money.'

Baby Richard was duly christened in April 1972, which meant another family gathering back in Wolverhampton at Lindum. Jane's brother, David, and Graham's sister, Maureen, were awarded roles as godparents. Five months later, in August 1972, Ian and Richard's first cousin (of 11, ultimately) arrived when Graham's 17 year old sister Susan gave birth to a baby boy named Robert. Graham's sister Maureen gave birth to the second cousin just over a year later in September 1973, a girl this time, named Emma, causing great delight as the first grand-daughter for Ernie and Ida. The families and their new babies would meet up at Graham's parents' home whenever the Hawkinses visited Wolverhampton.

The 1972/73 season saw a downward shift in Preston's fortunes - home crowds had more than halved from over 20,000 to less than 10,000 and Ball was sacked in February 1973. Fans held protests against the directors of the club, whom they believed were guilty of mismanagement and there was a failed takeover attempt by local businessmen. Frank Lord took over as manager for the remaining months of the season, but the players weren't happy. Graham said of Lord: 'There certainly wasn't the depth of thought on the tactical side as there was with Bally, and he had players playing out of their usual positions which wasn't needed and very confusing. Spav was also frozen out which didn't go down well at all.' 'Spav' was good friend and midfielder Alan Spavin, who made over 400 appearances for Preston. Ball had been a popular manager with the players, who had engendered a positive team spirit amongst them all. Jane's brother David had also enjoyed his tenure, joining Graham and the team on the bus for some away games. Graham held 'Bally' in great esteem, and was sad to see him go. He'd had a mild heart attack at the end of the previous season and his heavy smoking had not really abated. Ball sadly died prematurely, but not due to the nicotine, rather he was tragically killed in a car accident in Cyprus aged just 57 in 1982.

Relegation to Division Three followed, and whilst the much-publicised arrival of the new manager for the 1973/74 season, legend Bobby Charlton, lifted spirits in the dressing room, football wasn't going well for Graham at this time. Family life was a welcome break, and Jane remembers: 'Graham always said coming home to us three was what kept him sane.' Bobby's brother and fellow World Cup winner Jack Charlton, then manager at Middlesbrough, sold Nobby Stiles, World Cup Winner, to Preston North End, and Bobby duly handed him the captain's armband. Jane doesn't remember Graham being particularly surprised or concerned by the loss of the captaincy - more of an issue for him was being asked to play out of position. January 1974 saw both Plymouth Argyle and Blackburn Rovers make offers for Graham and the time felt right to make a move. Graham said of this time, 'To be fair I wasn't enjoying my football much and couldn't seem to ever really please the management. I was being asked to play in midfield at times which just wasn't me. There was no way I was upping sticks and going to Plymouth, so after agreeing it all at home, Rovers it was. It turned out to be a good move for me personally, and Gordon Lee was good to work with. I was back in the middle of defence, the manager believed in me, we won the Third Division title in 74/75 and I enjoyed my time there.'

After six years at Preston, it was time for Graham to move on, and Blackburn was an easy choice given it was only ten miles west of Deepdale, so the family could stay in their home in Lytham - time for a new footballing chapter.

A MARRIAGE MADE IN FOOTBALL

Graham models the catering offering available for the Blackburn players in the mid-seventies. Fourth in line is team-mate Tony Parkes.

4 By Skill and Hard Work

1974 – 1978 Lytham Part Two

The seventies have a distinctive 'look'. Sideburns, flares, kipper ties, flowery shirts, brown and orange swirly carpets. John Travolta in Saturday Night Fever, lorry loads of rubbish lining the streets of London due to striking bin-men, IRA violence. Despite, or perhaps in opposition to, the increasing prominence of feminist writers such as Germaine Greer, it feels like a testosterone-fuelled, masculine decade. For Jane and Graham, though, life in the sea-side town of Lytham during these years was mostly blissful and fun. Graham was at the peak of his playing career, bouncing baby boys arrived safely and life was good. Pre-season tours took Graham to Northern Ireland as well as the Republic of Ireland, and Jane did worry whilst he was away, but for the young family, these were mostly untroubled times. Graham particularly enjoyed listening to the music in the pubs of Ireland, Jane tells me.

Like Preston, Blackburn was an historic club, founded in 1875 by cotton mill managers and was also one of the 12 founding members of the English Football League. The 2020 Netflix series, The English Game, features the story of Fergie Suter, a Blackburn Rovers player from the era of the birth of the modern game. Suter was reportedly the first known professional player in what was originally an amateur sport and the series tells a great tale of Blackburn's role in England's early football history.

When Graham signed in June 1974, the club had been out of the top flight for 18 years and had fallen to Division Three in 1971. The club's highlight of the sixties was reaching an FA Cup final against Graham's old club Wolves in 1960. Blackburn were reduced to ten men for the second half, after full back Dave Whelan[5] broke his leg (substitutes only allowed from 1965), and went on to lose 3-0. Derek Dougan, Graham's team-mate at Wolves and room-mate during his time playing for LA Wolves, had played in that final for Blackburn, but he lost the faith of many Blackburn supporters when it came out that he had handed in a transfer request the day before. Dougan lasted just one more season at Blackburn and after spells at Aston Villa, Peterborough and Leicester he joined up with Wolves and Graham in 1967, where he enjoyed his greatest success (and notoriety) as a player.

Dougan wasn't the only former team-mate of Graham's to have had a spell at Blackburn. Next-door neighbour, former Wolves team-mate and business partner in the garage, midfielder Ken Knighton had also played for Blackburn a few years after Dougan's departure, when a near bankrupt Preston had sold him for £40,000[6] in 1969, taking on the captaincy in short order. Knighton didn't stay long however, as Blackburn suffered the blight of declining gate revenues and needing the funds, in 1971 he was sold for £60,000 to Hull City.

Whilst Dougan reputedly did not enjoy his time at Ewood Park, 13 years after he left, Jane and Graham easily settled into life at the club in 1974 and found it warm and welcoming. From when Richard was around two years old, Jane would take the boys to watch their Dad play at home games, meeting up with other players' wives in the '100 Club' which was just opposite the ground at Ewood Park. She would take some snacks and soup in a flask for the boys, Richard and Ian would yell 'Daddy!' when they saw him come out on to the pitch and Graham would do a secret 'wave', scratching behind his ear to acknowledge his most loyal fans. The 100 Club had been established in 1971 by the then incoming chairman, William Bancroft. Jane remembers Wiliam and his wife were very sociable, often inviting players to their home. Jane, Richard and Ian all remember the 100 Club as a fun, welcoming place, but as well as providing a social environment for players and fans, it was also a fund-raising club, granting members of the club access to the players in return for a subscription.

BY SKILL AND HARD WORK

Jane and Graham met Blackburn superfan, Joe Mercer (no, not the former Everton manager) at the 100 Club, and he would go on to become a lifelong friend. Joe was born in Great Harwood, neighbour to Blackburn, but after a career in the RAF, he had settled in Cornwall with partner Gwen. The pair ran a pub, The Fourways Inn, with several guest rooms. A passionate Blackburn fan, Joe would drive up hundreds of miles from Cornwall in his sports car to every home game, and mingle with the players in the 100 Club after matches. Joe invited Graham and fellow players to spend the summer in his pub in St Minver, and they would all head down with their families for a week of splashing around in Joe's pool and exploring the local beaches in Rock, Polzeath and Daymer Bay. Jane remembers eating mackerel in the pub, taking the ferry to Padstow and playing games on the beach. Gwen was a wonderful host and often prepared fresh crab for her guests, now a favourite of Jane's. Gwen was also housekeeper to then Poet Laureate, Sir John Betjeman, who lived nearby. One of Betjeman's poems, Greenaway, describes the walk much frequented and loved by the Hawkins family, from Polzeath to Daymer Bay. Richard remembers running with his Dad along this path, so beautifully described by Betjeman:

I know so well this turfy mile,
These clumps of sea-pink withered brown,
The breezy cliff, the awkward stile,
The sandy path that takes me down.

Sadly Joe died in 2005, and their bungalow and pool are no longer there, having been bulldozed and new houses built on the site, but The Fourways Inn is still around, now run by Joe's son Jamie.

Graham's younger brother Andrew, 12 years old when Graham joined Blackburn, also has fond memories of Graham's time at Deepdale: 'My biggest memories of Graham's playing career were probably when he played for Blackburn Rovers. My Dad, Mom and myself would sometimes stay at Graham and Jane's for a week when they lived in Lytham St Anne's and a couple of times I went with Graham when he had training and watched - that is when I got hooked on football. I can't explain the pride I felt when I watched him play - it was amazing.' Blackburn fans soon got behind their new signing, and one in particular, was inspired to name his son Graham after watching him play. During lockdown, BBC Lancashire DJ Graham Liver (and former Blackburn Rovers reporter) revealed on air that he was named after his father's childhood hero, prompting sons Ian and Richard to drop him a line to say how his revelation had brought a smile to Mum Jane's face.

Graham started studying for his FA coaching badges whilst at Blackburn, planning for his career after he retired from playing. The FA run coaching courses for both professional footballers as well as amateur enthusiasts who want to coach kids on a Sunday morning, covering basic drills initially, culminating in developing tactical training sessions for 11 v 11 as part of the final qualification for today's aspiring professional managers. Back in the seventies, there was no requirement for a manager's qualification, but Graham wanted to learn. The course involved spending a couple of weeks down at The FA in Lilleshall, and was an opportunity for Graham to get together with other players and coaches and share tips on all aspects of managing a professional football team. Today, the final qualification requires a number of hours coaching experience. Whilst not a requirement at that time, Graham had nonetheless started amassing hours with his involvement in the Sunday League Piper team. Toddler Ian also played his part in Graham's early coaching experience, becoming the Piper's official team mascot once he turned two. Graham enjoyed coaching, and his leadership qualities had been much in evidence whilst captain at Preston and so football management seemed to be a viable option once his playing career was over. Nevertheless, Graham and Jane were always aware that a career in football was likely to be precarious, and this realisation meant that Jane's original desire of having four children was quietly dropped. She had seen how tough it had been for Graham's parents Ernest and Ida, raising four children with limited means, and was starting to enjoy some of the trappings of being financially comfortable.

The boys were healthy and happy. Jane enjoyed motherhood and found that her boys were a catalyst to overcoming the shyness she'd felt in younger years. Young Richard did give his parents a minor scare, though. When he started walking, Jane noticed that one of his legs didn't seem to be formed properly. No one could remember which leg, but after going back to cine camera footage, it seemed it was the left leg. As is the football way, Richard was taken to the club doctor who referred him to an orthopaedic surgeon. A plaster cast was put on his leg to try and encourage it to grow straight, but when it was removed there seemed to be no difference. The same procedure was repeated, the cast more securely applied and another month later, the problem seemed to be solved. Uncle David remembers leaving the ground one time with Graham carrying Richard in his cast when fans asked for his autograph. 'He'd always stop and sign them.' David remembers, 'He'd say: "you know your career's over when they stop asking".'

Four of Graham and Jane's siblings got married in the seventies: Graham's sisters Susan and Maureen married Harry and Bill respectively in 1972, Jane's brothers David and Robert married Angela and Diane in 1975. There are many photographs of Ian and Richard in some wonderful matching outfits from these occasions - friend Chris' boutique shop in Lytham was often the source of a fine selection of Rupert Bear trousers and flowery shirts. It is possible that this was the seed of Ian's love of flamboyant shirts, but it didn't rub off on Richard - it could be that his younger age led him to be more influenced by conservative eighties styling. Jane was a fan of seventies fashion: 'Graham did wear flared trousers, flowered 'kipper' ties and suits with massive lapels. I loved the floaty colourful tops, flares, hot pants. I had a trouser suit made in cotton with a type of paisley pattern all over, loved it.' With the football connections ever-present in the Hawkins household, shopping for sportswear for the boys took Jane to Lancaster, where Preston team-mates Alan Spavin and Alan Kelly, the Irish international goal keeper had a shop, offering discounts for friends naturally.

After the four weddings, sadly there was to be a funeral. In the summer of 1976, Graham's mother, Ida, had gone into hospital for a routine gall bladder operation, and whilst she returned home to convalesce, she never fully recovered and died shortly afterwards. Jane's father, Samuel, after visiting Ida, alerted the unsuspecting Graham as to the seriousness of his mother's condition. Returning early from a pre-season tour in Gibraltar, Graham dashed back to Wolverhampton to see her, but was sadly too late. The news was devastating for all of the family, but particularly 14 year old Andrew, who came to spend some time in Lytham with his big brother Graham in the aftermath of Ida's passing. Just a few months later in December 1976, Ian and Richard's third cousin arrived, Maureen's second child, whom she named Andrew after his uncle, her younger brother. It must have been a bitter-sweet time for Maureen, so soon after losing her mother. Jane remembers the joy that the latest arrival brought: 'Andrew was always a very happy smiley boy, everyone loved him.'

In an age where nappies were washed as disposable nappies were mostly unreliable, Richard and Ian had to be toilet trained before Jane would take them away on holiday. Ian had been taken to Hotel Bahia del Este in Cala Millor, Majorca in the summer of 1972 with Richard deposited at Lindum for a holiday in Wolverhampton with Jane's parents. Richard did not have to wait long for his first plane ride though - as well as the Cornwall pad, Blackburn fan Joe Mercer also had a holiday home in Malta that all four Hawkins visited in the summer of 1975. With their Lytham home empty for a week, brother David and new wife Angela took advantage and enjoyed their honeymoon by the sea. The Blackburn years saw return holidays to both St Minver and Malta in the off-season in June; when the boys reached school age Jane would take them out of school for a week or so to make sure that they all got to spend the time together, as Graham would be back in pre-season training by the time the school summer holidays came around.

Jane remembers a great team spirit at Blackburn and each season Graham was there, the team outperformed the last. Blackburn had been stuck in Division Three since 1972, coming close but not quite doing enough to secure promotion to Division Two, but the season Graham joined signalled the beginning of a turnaround in the club's fortunes as well as the approaching centenary of the club in 1975. Gordon Lee, having been appointed as Blackburn's manager in January 1974, was looking to halt their decline and set about recruiting the kind of players he thought could do it. In Blackburn fan and accountant Harry Berry's epic history of Blackburn, 'A Century of Soccer: 1875 - 1975', he describes what Lee wanted: 'he required players who were willing to sweat blood for Blackburn Rovers. Character and ability, the will to win, and confidence without narcissism, were the qualities he looked for.' Graham certainly fitted the bill and the Blackburn motto of 'by skill and hard work' sat well with him. Berry certainly believes that Lee did good business when Blackburn acquired him, describing him as: 'the blond, unyielding Preston centre-half who was destined to display the kind of form that made his previous employers appear misguided philanthropists in accepting a fee of £18,000.'

As well as Graham, Lee brought in Ken Beamish, Pat Hilton, Graham Oates, Don Hutchins and Jimmy Mullen, and sold on players he believed would detract from his vision. He had to operate within tight budget constraints, but bought well according to Berry, who describes Hutchins' purchase for £10,000 as 'a piece of effrontery equatable to the capture of Hawkins'. The club finished 13th in the Third Division in 1974, one point above Plymouth Argyle, the club Graham had rejected due to its location on the south coast. Lee's first full season, 1974/75, duly delivered Graham's second turn-around season and the team won promotion to Division Two - Graham becoming Division Three Champions for a second time. Graham spoke fondly of Lee and how he developed Graham's game to 'play out from the back' - in an interview with the Lancashire Telegraph Graham said: 'Gordon was a great influence. I'd been brought up at Wolverhampton Wanderers and I was a defender who went to head it, stopped people from scoring, and kicked the ball up the other end of the field. So I had the shock of my life when I had my first training session at Altham and Gordon set it up, with Roger[7] in goal and the back four, and he said, "right, this is how we're going to play". He turned round to myself and said: "you're going to get the ball off Roger" and I went blank. Nobody had asked me to do that before. But that was how we played, that was Gordon and nobody else. It took time but he was very patient and as long as everybody did their very best, he'd take the mistakes, but if anybody ducked and dived, they'd get a bit of a hammering.' Berry concurs that the coaching Lee provided, had a significant impact on Graham's game: 'Hawkins, the dour stopper of Preston memory, was given free rein to move upfield and display a precision and flair in using the ball that few could have guessed he possessed. To foster the belief that they were a footballing side, the aimless hoof upfield was eliminated in favour of 'patience' football.'

Graham met close friend Derek Fazackerley ('Faz') and defensive partner at Blackburn, and wife Chris likewise became a good friend to Jane. Faz would go on to spend all of his playing career at Blackburn, playing a record of 671 games for his club and is still their most-capped player. At the time of Graham's arrival he was just 22 and still trying to make his way in the game. Faz had grown up in Preston and was an avid football fan - he'd watched Graham from the terraces in Deepdale as a young man. Graham was an experienced player, joining Blackburn just before his 28th birthday and Faz looked up to him: 'Graham was a great mentor and friend to me.' Faz had been competing for his place in the team with John Waddington, but a goal against Charlton, set-up by Graham, sealed Faz as first choice in the title-winning 1974/75 season. Berry describes the build-up in his book: 'the first goal after 40 minutes stemmed from a combination move between centre backs Hawkins and Fazackerley. It followed a left-wing corner from Mullen. Tutt, the elastoline Charlton goalkeeper, hurtled out, to prevent Parkes getting in a header, missed the ball, but collided with the Rovers' player, leaving both men on the ground. His centre-half Goldthorpe turned the ball away but only as far as Hawkins patrolling the mid-field area. The big man steadied himself, spotted Fazackerley wide on the right and chipped in an inch-perfect ball over the defender, leaving Fazackerley clear but still outside the area…'

Graham and Faz went on to become great friends, playing together as numbers 5 and 6, rooming together when the team was on tour. Graham would pick Faz up on the way to training and the pair would be sounding boards for each other on their shared car journeys. Faz remembered the first time he and his then girlfriend, now wife, Chris, visited the Hawkinses in Lytham, whilst walking Faz's parents' dog, Rusty. Still keen to impress his new defensive partner, Faz was mortified to see Rusty cock his leg at their open door, and duly mark his territory. Unsurprisingly, Graham and Jane just laughed.

In an interview with the Lancashire Telegraph, Faz shared some insight on a February 1975 fixture between Blackburn Rovers and Plymouth Argyle, voted by the paper's readers as the stand-out game of the seventies. Plymouth Argyle were Blackburn's main rival for the top spot in the league and also achieved promotion in 1975, finishing behind Blackburn in second. Blackburn were 0-2 down at half-time, but made a superb comeback: 'I can remember myself and my centre back partner Graham Hawkins being distraught at half-time because we both thought we'd played like a pair of absolute wallies. We managed to turn it around and win 5-2, but I can still remember me and Graham thinking after the game, "We'd better improve this or we're not going to get promoted!" But we were a good side. We played some decent football. As downbeat as you are when you get relegated, to get promoted after three or four years of trying was tremendous. We weren't the biggest team in the league, not by any means, but Blackburn were one of the founder members and to get them back into the Second Division was a big achievement. I think there was a general feeling that we shouldn't have been in the Third Division.'

As well as winning the league in 1975, Graham also had the honour of being named in the PFA (Professional Footballers' Association, the players' trade union) Division Three team of the year, alongside two of his Blackburn team-mates in defence, Andy Burgin and Roger Jones the goalkeeper. The award was first presented in 1974 and the shortlist is compiled by the members of the PFA, with the winners then being voted for by the other players in their respective divisions.

Blackburn took their players off to Benidorm at the end of the 1974/75 season to celebrate winning the league. For Faz, this was only the second time he'd been abroad, and whilst Graham had been on a few overseas trips, for many of the younger players, it was a new experience. One player, Bobby Hoy, after getting sunburnt and spending a couple of days in bed recovering, was excited to be back out with the boys and started boxing a cardboard cutout of a chef outside a cafe. The cutout, at about five foot seven or eight, was a similar height to the diminutive player. One Spanish policeman, sensing trouble, was not amused and pulled his gun out. Graham, ever the peace-maker, stepped up to try and diffuse the situation, only to find the gun pressed into his ribs. Thankfully, language barriers aside, all lived to tell the tale. Another player keen to make the most of the sun, after the seemingly endless Lancashire rain, was Jimmy Mullen. Faz remembers a group of players helping him to take the plaster cast off his healing broken leg, to ensure an even tan.

Initially, training took place at Altham, pitches that the club leased for a couple of years, at the back of the Accrington Stanley ground to the east of Blackburn. Faz remembers that the facilities were woefully inadequate, 'Even the year we went up under Gordon Lee it seemed to rain and rain and I can hardly remember training on a grass pitch. We used to train at Altham on an old shail tennis court.' There were football pitches at Altham, but with incessant rain from October to March they were mostly flooded and impossible to play on, the shale underneath the grass cutting the players' knees to shreds. Most of the time they trained on tennis courts. The lease at Altham was not renewed and Faz remembers they had to 'beg, steal and borrow' grass pitches to train on, which at times meant ringing local schools. The first team would train on council-owned pitches at Pleasington to the West of Blackburn on the Thursdays before a match, right up until the moment when Jack Walker invested in Blackburn in 1988. Walker provided the funds to build the current training facilities in Brockhall Village, to the north of Blackburn in the picturesque Ribble Valley.

Whilst much of football life in the seventies was not very glamorous, that's not to say there weren't parties for the players. Faz remembers that Graham was eager to ensure the team socialised together with partners and families, keen to foster team spirit. The Pipers club in Preston was also a favourite haunt of the Blackburn players as well as those from Preston North End: 'We had some of our best meetings in there,' laughs Faz. Christmas parties would include wives and girlfriends, and would be held in local pubs or hotels, for a meal, drinks 'and a good old sing-song.'

Lee was tempted away from Blackburn after winning the league, and impatient to try his hand at management at the top flight, he left to join First Division team, Newcastle United, taking his assistant Richard Dinnis with him. Jim Smith, a Sheffield man nicknamed the Bald Eagle (for no other reason other than his hair-free head, it would appear, 'slightly less hair when he left,' laughed Faz), took up the reins at Blackburn soon after, bringing in his assistant Norman Bodell and John Pickering as Reserves team coach. In their first season in Division Two under Smith, the team finished a respectable 15th, although it had been a difficult start, with Graham and a number of other players suffering injuries. Lee would ultimately tempt a number of his Blackburn team to join him in Newcastle, including Graham's team-mate and friend, Graham Oates. It was another good season for Graham though, unanimously voted Player's Player of the Year at the end of the season, narrowly missing out on the Fan's Player of the Year by just one vote - the award went to team-mate Tony Parkes.

In 1976 Smith bought Gordon Taylor from Birmingham City. Gordon was appointed chairman of the PFA in 1978, succeeding Derek Dougan, funnily enough, and went on to be the PFA's chief executive for over 40 years, since retiring from professional football in 1980. Gordon became a helpful connection for the Hawkinses over the years. Also joining Blackburn in 1976, was Graham's former Wolves team-mate, Dave Wagstaffe. 'Waggy' had been a key part of the Wolves team, making over 500 appearances between 1964 and 1976, always a serious threat on the wing and a wonderful passer of the ball. In talking to Clive Corbett, Graham recalled playing again with his team-mate from Wolves: 'I played with Waggy at Blackburn, he was a revelation there, him on the left side and Gordon Taylor on the right. They had doted on Bryan Douglas[8] and on his first home start without any back lift he clipped a ball from one side of Ewood Park to the other. I can hear the gasp now, the crowd loved him.' Waggy also entered the footballing history books for a less welcome award, being the first player to be awarded a red card after their formal introduction in October 1976. In November 1976, Graham and Waggy returned to Molineux to face their former team-mates, after Wolves had been relegated to Division Two for just the one season. Young Andrew, at the tender age of 14, went to the match with Dad Ernie: 'My best and unforgettable time was at Molineux when Blackburn played Wolves.

A MARRIAGE MADE IN FOOTBALL

Me and my Dad went to watch. Blackburn won 2-1 and Graham marked John Richards, out of the game. He was tremendous that day.'

Smith, like Graham and indeed Taylor and Waggy, would stay at Blackburn for a further two seasons, and would leave seeing Blackburn pushing for promotion to the top flight, finishing 12th in 1976/77 and 5th in 1977/78. Like his predecessor Lee, Smith wanted a shot at management in the top tier, and left to take a job at First Division Birmingham City in 1978, following the retirement of former England manager, Alf Ramsay. Faz remembers Blackburn as a well-run club, attracting high quality managers and whilst many had ambitions to manage clubs with bigger wallets, and so would only hang around for a few seasons, there was a consistent focus on playing entertaining football.

In 1977, Graham turned 31 and started to turn his thoughts towards the next phase of his career, knowing his playing days would soon be over. Smith had signed central defender Glen Keeley in 1976, who was some six years younger than Graham and effectively replaced him. By the time he left Blackburn, Graham had made 131 first-team appearances, but in his last season at the club, he was increasingly competing for his place and playing more games for the reserves. Alan Durban, then player-manager at Shrewsbury Town had been trying to persuade Graham to make a move to Third Division Shrewsbury Town, but Graham had resisted, holding out for a coaching role. In January 1978, an opportunity came up at Port Vale, where former Blackburn manager Gordon Lee had had his first managerial post in 1968-74. Graham switched clubs for a transfer fee of £6,000, taking on a role as player-coach under manager Bobby Smith. Good friend, former Blackburn team-mate and prolific striker Ken Beamish ('Beamo' to the Ewood Park faithful) had also joined Port Vale just over a year earlier in September 1976, for a transfer fee of £12,000.

Port Vale Football Club is situated in a small town called Burslem to the north of Stoke, an area known for its pottery industry. Over eighty miles from Lytham St Annes, this move meant a new home for the Hawkins family. Good friends Jenny and Ray were now based in Barlaston to the south of Stoke - Ray had got to know the area whilst working as a salesman selling hair products and gone on to buy a few salons - and were a great help in the house hunt, hosting the Hawkinses for a weekend of house-hunting and scouring the local newspapers for suitable properties. Football moves quickly, house moves less so, and for a while, Graham stayed in digs provided by Port Vale, a short walk from the ground. Jane and the boys would travel from Lytham to watch home games, and look at houses afterwards. Ultimately Graham picked out the winning house from the paper, and went to look at it one day after training. Three Westfields Rise was a five-bedroomed detached house in the village of Woore, thirty minutes to the west of Burslem, sitting on the borders of Shropshire, Cheshire and Staffordshire. A bank manager and his wife had been the first owners of the house, had only lived there 18 months so all of the fixtures and fittings were more or less new. The house had a family bathroom as well as an ensuite attached to the master bedroom, representing the epitome of luxury in 1978. It was 'the one' . The Hawkinses were set to enter the eighties in style, at least on the home front.

A MARRIAGE MADE IN FOOTBALL

Blackburn Rovers team holidays in St Minver with Joe Mercer. Adults from L to R: Joe, Graham, Joe's partner Gwen, Sue and Roger Jones (goalkeeper), John Waddington, Norman Bodell (coach), Jane, Mick Heaton (captain of 1975 league champions side), Val Waddington, Lois Bodell, Maureen Heaton, Faz and wife Chris, Joe's son Jamie and Neil Wilkinson. Richard and Ian are in the dinghy on the right.

5 A Brief Foray into the Fourth Division

1978 – 1980 Woore

The Hawkins family move down the M6 to the village of Woore came at the back end of the seventies, a decade known for the disruption of successive strikes, culminating in the 1978/79 'Winter of Discontent'. An exceptionally cold winter was accompanied by vast swathes of the working population going on strike to seek higher pay, with the success of one group fuelling inflation and inspiring others to seek still higher increases. Gravediggers, bin-men, lorry drivers, Ford workers and many others downed tools, ultimately leading to the downfall of James Callaghan and his Labour government, paving the way for Margaret Thatcher to number ten Downing Street in May 1979. For the Hawkins family, the eighties signalled the end of Graham's playing career, and the start of an eventful career in football management. Life as a football manager would take the family to live in a country they'd barely heard of for most of the Thatcher years, on the back of a roller-coaster time in the spotlight as manager of Wolverhampton Wanderers. But first, Port Vale.

Port Vale, Graham's fourth club, were also founder members of a football league - League Division Two in 1892 - and hold the infamous record of playing the most seasons of league football without ever breaking through into the top tier. Other than light shone by their celebrity super-fan, Robbie Williams, 'The Valiants' tend to live in the shadow of their bigger, more successful neighbour, Stoke City, another of the 'Twelve'. Graham's former boss, Gordon Lee, had spent six years as manager of Port Vale, before taking the job at Blackburn in 1974, earning himself a reputation for skilful management with limited funds, the then chairman Mark Singer saying Lee had 'done a wonderful job with little or no money'. Jeff Kent, author of a number of books on Port Vale, describes the period preceding Graham's arrival at the club in Chapter Ten of his book, The Valiants' Years, as: Surviving on a Shoestring: 1969 - 1979. Graham must have spoken to Lee about his time at Port Vale, and would have known some of the difficulties he would face there, but he wouldn't have expected that former Port Vale chairman, Arthur McPherson, would go on to describe the 1979/80 season as: 'probably the worst season in the club's history.' Jane and Graham were about to experience some of their hardest times in the football world. I asked Kent if he remembered Graham playing for Port Vale: 'Yes, I remember seeing Graham playing. He was a little long in the tooth as a player by then, but I could see that he had experience, skill and vision and he more than held his own despite coming to the end of his career.'

At Port Vale Graham played pretty much every match, including a 1-0 win away against Hereford on 23 March 1978 where he set up the winning goal with a well-placed free-kick, before struggling off the pitch after 31 minutes with flu symptoms. He'd signed himself off as fit and started the game when he probably should have been tucked up in bed with a Lemsip. The Hawkins family took up residence in Woore in May 1978, four months after Graham's move, in time for Ian and Richard to start the new year at the village school in September. The move coincided with the end of the 1977/78 football season and with Port Vale finishing 21st in Division Three, duly relegated to the Fourth Division.

Jane remembers going to the last home match, the penultimate game of the season, against Colchester on 24th April. Graham's first goal for Port Vale on 12 April, a last minute equaliser against Wrexham, gave the team a vital life-line but it wasn't enough. Port Vale's woeful goal difference meant that it was a must-win game against Colchester in order to avoid relegation, but the team, full of panic, went on to lose 3-0. Jane shed a tear at their plight, wailing 'I don't want to be in the Fourth Division…' - it felt like a step too far.

A BRIEF FORAY INTO THE FOURTH DIVISION

Jane describes the Port Vale experience in the Fourth Division as a 'real downgrade', and the numbers watching games were considerably diminished. Graham had played to crowds of over 50,000 whilst at Wolves, and whilst Preston and Blackburn were smaller clubs, Port Vale's Fourth Division crowd was less than 10,000, sometimes as low as a couple of thousand. After being relegated, Graham's boss and manager Bobby Smith duly left in May 1978 to take up the post as Swindon Town manager, claiming: 'People may say that I am deserting a sinking ship, but that is not the case,' although with hindsight, Port Vale's trajectory was most definitely downwards. Port Vale demanded Swindon compensate them for their loss of their manager to the tune of £10,500. Graham later said that those months together in 1978 had been valuable experience: 'I was youth coach under Bobby Smith and learned a lot from it.' Smith's assistant, Dennis Butler was promoted to manager and Graham became his assistant manager. With just six months' experience as an assistant manager after finishing his playing career, Butler, like Graham, was in the early stages of learning his craft. One of Graham's new roles as assistant manager was acting as Butler's chauffeur as he'd lost his license for drink-driving, picking him up from Lower Tean, a village to the east of Burslem, effectively doubling Graham's daily commute time. Coincidentally, many years later, friends Jenny and Ray moved into the house next door to Dennis and his wife Cynthia.

Fortunately, on the domestic front, the move to Woore was an unqualified success and the family quickly took to village life there, making friends with the neighbours and getting involved with the rich community social life. The village school was small, with only three classes - one for all of the infants where six-year old Richard started, and two classes for the junior-aged children, the younger grouping of which Ian joined aged eight. Having enjoyed working in the school kitchens in Lytham, Jane started her job hunt at Woore Primary School, and although at the time of asking, there were no vacancies, headmaster Brian Gibbons called in September 1978 to ask Jane if she still wanted a job. The kitchen assistant was leaving to go on maternity leave and Jane accepted the post happily. There were three women in the kitchen, Mrs Jones, head cook, along with Jane and Ada Bailey. Mrs Jones and Ada's family grew the fruit and vegetables at the school and brought them in for her team to prepare. It all sounds straight out of the sitcom, 'The Good Life'. Jane describes her initial post as 'third in charge general dogsbody', but within two years she was operating as head cook, once Mrs Jones retired. It was Ada who suggested Jane start writing a diary - as a keen vegetable-grower, she kept a daily record of activities, but also the weather to monitor the impact on their produce. Jane kept detailed records throughout the eighties - a great help in compiling this memoir.

Woore was in easy reach of a cluster of towns known as the Staffordshire Potteries, collectively famous for ceramic production since the 17th Century. The family would go to Hanley for shopping and cinema - Jane also enjoyed shopping at the independent shops in Market Drayton as well as the Wednesday market there. Sadly the days of the boys' matching outfits had come to an end, as they began to insist on choosing their own clothes. Graham, ever the snappy dresser, liked to get his suits and casual clothes from a store in Nantwich.

Ian and Richard's footballing careers began in Woore, initially through the 'Lads and Dads League'. Ladsandads was set up in 1967 by Doug Brown, Stoke City physiotherapist and future mayor, and grew into an organised league for all schoolboys initially in the Staffordshire area, including those who might not make it into a school team, with matches held on school pitches at weekends. Ladsandads is still going strong today in Staffordshire for both boys and girls, run collectively with the support of Dads (and presumably open to Mums too!), with the over-riding principle that every player gets at least half a game. Brown was inspired by England's World Cup win in 1966 and wanted to ensure that all boys got the chance to play football. Through an advert in Hanley-based paper, The Sentinel, Brown invited Dads to bring their sons to Trentham Park to gauge the level of interest. Players such as the Chamberlain brothers Mark and Neville started out their footballing careers playing Ladsandads football, before getting signed by Port Vale and going on to become professional footballers, in Mark's case, at international level. Both Chamberlain brothers were starting their first team careers when Graham started at Port Vale, making their debuts in 1977 and 1978, and Jane remembers them fondly. Richard remembers being mesmerised by Mark Chamberlain walking all the way round the pitch, keeping the ball up all the way.

Graham and his sons' involvement in Ladsandads came about through friend Roger Jones, goalkeeper and team-mate at Blackburn (1970-76). Jones had moved to Stoke in 1977, and his son played in the Ladsandads league, for Loggerhead Lions, a local team that Richard would later play for. The Hawkins boys' first team was Madeley Bears, based in a village three miles up the road from Woore. Initially just Ian played, as at just six years old, Richard was deemed too young. However, having filled in a few times when the team was short, he soon became an under-aged regular, but 'he had to go on the team sheet as 'AN Other',' Jane remembers. The boys didn't enjoy success at first, but Graham tapped into what would motivate them: 'Graham took over the duties of managing the team with other dads who we got on well with. The team played many games without even scoring a goal. Graham promised them all pop and crisps when they got a goal and it was as though they had won the cup when they scored.' Graham also turned his hand to act as referee, although handling the parents off the pitch was usually the greater challenge. Jane remembers one such occasion: 'A lot of the parents gave their kids a hard time if they didn't do well. One day one mum was yelling at the ref who was Graham, so he stopped the game walked over to her and offered her the whistle. She then shut up.' The boys also played school team matches. Headmaster Mr Gibbons also had three sons who played football and Jane and Graham got to know him through lift-sharing on the way to matches - henceforth affectionately known as 'Gibbo'. The younger Hawkins' success on the football field came at Buckley Hall, a children's home in the village that held an annual fête in the gardens, which one year included a junior school 5-a-side tournament. Both Ian and Richard played for the Woore school team and proudly lifted their first ever football trophy together.

Like many boys growing up in the seventies, Ian and Richard joined the cub scouts, meeting every week in Woore Victory Hall. Jane's friend Ann Coupe's mother Mary was the second-in-command cub leader, her husband one of the scout leaders - a true family affair. Ian went on to join the scouts aged ten and a half and played football for them, but for Richard, after his stint in the cubs and achieving his swimming badges, playing football was all he wanted to do. In contrast, whilst Ian always played a lot of football, he has always been open to trying a multitude of activities, which in adult life include triathlons, open water swims, marathons, three peaks challenge, magic circle and so on. In the summer of 1980, the Hawkins boys enjoyed their first cub camp. Jane and Graham took full advantage of their chance of freedom and enjoyed a few days' child-free holiday in Lytham, staying with friends and former neighbours, Chris and Dave.

Port Vale's new season under Butler started off with a three-match tour of Scotland, with unconvincing results. If Graham and Jane thought relegation to the Fourth Division was bad, unfortunately the season of 1978/79 would prove to be calamitous. Butler had big plans to turn around Port Vale's fortunes, and went on to smash club record transfer fees for both selling and buying players, carrying out a massive overhaul of the team. Butler's big signings, in particular Ken Todd (£37,000, smashing the previous club record of £15,000) and Peter Farrell (£40,000, breaking the club record a second time in one season) failed to deliver on the pitch and the fans' fury grew, much of it directed at Farrell and Todd. Chris Harper, long-serving football reporter at the Hanley-based Sentinel newspaper asked: 'Have the board gone berserk after years of frugal existence?', but chairman Arthur McPherson was unrepentant, believing: 'We are going places.'

Lytham friend and former Blackburn team-mate Ken Beamish had been named Player of the Year the previous season by the Port Vale fans, on account of his 16 goals making him top scorer (adding to his 18 goals from the previous season), but Port Vale dispensed with his services, selling him to Third Division Bury for £35,000. Another former Player of the Year (1975/76), John Ridley, was sold to Leicester City for £55,000 and there were a number of other ins and outs, including £30,000 spent on Bob Delgado who made his debut at centre half on Boxing Day 1978, alongside Graham and Gerry Keenan, at right back. That game, away at Barnsley, would be another opportunity for Graham to meet his old schoolboy team-mate, Allan Clarke, then player-manager at Barnsley. Allan had achieved a great deal in his footballing career, scoring the winning goal at the 1972 FA

A BRIEF FORAY INTO THE FOURTH DIVISION

Cup Final at Wembley for Leeds United, for whom he scored 110 goals over seven years. Sadly for Graham, it was to be another heavy defeat in which Allan scored a hat-trick and helped Barnsley on to a 6-2 win. Kent describes the situation at the end of that sorry match: 'In four months, 13 players had featured in deals involving almost £250,000 and at a net loss to the club of £32,000. It was therefore not a happy party that left fourth-placed Barnsley on Boxing Day after the Valiants had been 'drubbed'.'

In the new year, Gordon Banks, former England goalkeeper and World Cup winner from 1966 was brought in as a coach at Port Vale for a while, which did seem to translate into improved defensive performances for a period, but they were not sustained. Banks went on to complain that the players 'just did not like hard work' when he left in December 1979. Before he died in 2019, Gordon together with Jane were part of a regular walking group in Trentham Gardens which includes a number of Stoke ex-footballers from the sixties and their 'WAGs'.

Violence occasionally spilled out onto the pitch, Butler labelled the fans 'a bunch of yobbos' and their relationship broke down irretrievably. The seventies had seen increasing violence on the football terraces across the UK, and Kent describes a number of violent incidents in The Valiants' Years in the early seventies, including mass brawls, bricks thrown at police and rival fans, snowballs lobbed at police and the rival goalkeeper. In April 1973 at a Bolton game, brick-hurling and pitch invasions culminated in the referee being 'bundled to the ground, kicked and carried off'. Back then, fans were not strictly segregated in grounds, and they would change ends at half-time, often leading to confrontation when they mixed. After a Blackpool fan was stabbed to death by a Bolton Wanderers fan in 1974, and increasing amounts of organised violence across a number of clubs, including Manchester United's infamous 'Red Army' of fans, The FA started to take action to enforce fan segregation. This included preventing fans from changing ends and building fences to prevent pitch invasions. In response to the trouble at the game against Bolton, Port Vale built their steel fence in front of the Bycars End at the start of the 1973/74 season.

Fighting wasn't restricted to the fans - in February 1974 a fracas broke out in the players' tunnel after a fight between opposing players on the pitch escalated. There were also repeated fines from The FA for poor conduct - in the seventies Port Vale had a reputation for notching up player bookings. Jane still took Richard and Ian to watch their Dad play at Vale Park in Burslem, but tried to shield them from some of the fans' taunts on the odd occasion they singled out Graham, which included 'Procters have better coaches' (Procters were a local bus company), 'I told the lads that the supporters were all mad,' Jane says. I asked Kent if he remembered any comments directed at Graham: 'I'd say it was almost inevitable that Jane would have heard comments like that because fans will have a go at anybody and everybody. I have no memory of Graham being singled out for abuse or even criticism, unlike I have of one or two unfortunate players. Indeed, my cousin, Harry Poole, the club's second-longest-serving player came in for criticism from fans from time to time, which led to arguments with our assembled family there!' Despite the rise in football hooliganism, having watched his Dad play regularly throughout the seventies and eighties, Richard doesn't recall witnessing any violence or pitch invasions - whilst there were some serious flare-ups, it wasn't the norm.

Port Vale didn't bounce straight back into Division Three in their 1978/79 season, rather they finished a lowly 16th in Division Four, conceding 70 goals. Kent describes how wages had more than doubled under Butler's tenure and the club made its biggest financial loss to date (£52,000). Mark Singer was sacked as club president in May 1979, with chairman McPherson refusing to comment. Rumours were rife of a series of bust-ups at board level, with arguments over finances and the repayment of directors' loans. The incumbent chairman Arthur McPherson had been replaced by Mark Singer as Port Vale chairman back in March 1970, after McPherson was found guilty of handling stolen goods (liquid gold used to decorate pottery), but McPherson was back in post in March 1977 with Mark Singer moving to become club president. McPherson remained as chairman until October 1980, when he resigned after a 'blaze of criticism'. Whilst sadly Graham isn't around to get his insights into that turbulent season at Port Vale, it certainly seems like it was a baptism of fire, and he must have welcomed having some time in the off-season to connect with family and friends in his new home in Woore.

Jane loved village life in Woore and easily made friends there. Another benefit of moving down from Lytham, was that they were that much closer to friends and family, as Jane remembers: 'It was lovely being closer to Wolverhampton so when Graham played away me and the boys would be over to see the family.' Graham's Dad and new wife Ann were near enough to come and babysit the boys on the odd occasion that Graham and Jane went out, 'they enjoyed those times and Ann had the patience to teach Ian to knit!'. They still kept in touch with friends they'd made in Lytham, with visits from Chris and Dave, their former neighbours, as well as Faz and wife Chris, kids in tow keeping the boys entertained. Friends from Blackburn were not forgotten either, and the family enjoyed more summer holidays down in St Minver in both 1979 and 1981.

Stan and Pauline, the friends Jane and Graham made during their trip to Margate in the early days of their courtship, lived only an hour away in Markfield, near Leicester, and they came over to visit in the summer of 1979. The friends had a fun evening, spending time in the Coopers Arms pub as well as visiting friends in the village. Seven year old Richard remembers being woken by some commotion in the middle of the night, seeing Stan standing by the open window of the guest bedroom, complaining of being unable to breathe, his parents in the room in their night-clothes. Jane remembers: 'We rang for an ambulance and our doctor and Graham had tried hard with artificial respiration.' Stan didn't make it - he died of a heart attack that night. The news was devastating, and the following day Graham and Jane did what they could to support Pauline. 'Pauline didn't drive so Graham drove Stan's car and I drove ours, to take them home,' said Jane. Their two children, ('Maria must have been 12 and Paul 10') were also staying with the Hawkinses, and it's hard to imagine the terrible burden of breaking the news to them.

Graham lost his good friend in terrible circumstances, a man in the prime of his life with a young family, and just three years after

A MARRIAGE MADE IN FOOTBALL

Graham had lost his mother. His return to Port Vale for the 1979/80 season did not bring any improvement in fortunes. Butler was sacked as manager in August 1979, and the club turned to former player and then youth team coach, Alan Bloor to act as caretaker manager rather than Graham. Furthermore, Graham was told there was no coaching role for him at the club and so was effectively dismissed. Port Vale wouldn't release Graham's player registration, so was unable to play elsewhere, leaving him with no option but to pursue an unfair dismissal claim. The PFA helped out with a lawyer, but Port Vale didn't engage with Graham's complaint, leaving Graham unable to earn any money from playing football, whilst waiting for the court process to take its course - with the hearing not set until April 1980, some seven months later.

At the time of Graham's departure from Port Vale in September 1979, the local paper, The Sentinel, were having their own spat with Port Vale over some of their reporting of troubles at the club. The Sentinel reported the club's line, namely that Graham had gone AWOL because Bloor had been given the top job, however Graham enjoyed a good relationship with his fellow coach and was aggrieved because he had been relieved of his coaching responsibilities by Port Vale, in breach of his contract. Jane remembers: 'it was an accumulation of events that led to the unfair dismissal.' Graham had taken Bloor's place on the England 'A' team tour back in 1969; it is typical of the world of football that Bloor would go on to take Graham's place as Port Vale's manager a decade later.

Kent, based on reports from the Sentinel at the time, describes the settlement of the case outside a court in Shrewsbury, stating that Graham: 'dropped his unfair dismissal claim in favour of a compensation offer an hour before an industrial tribunal was due to meet to decide the matter', implying Graham had refused to engage in discussions with Port Vale, when in fact the opposite was true. The press reported the tribunal chairman, Anthony Gordon, as somewhat disappointed that the case had been settled, 'We always find our more interesting cases get settled. It might have been quite interesting.' Graham's lawyer, Clement Goldstone (went on to become a judge based in Liverpool) retorted with a laugh, 'We are sorry to have disappointed you. I am sure we can arrange for you to have his autograph.' Graham wasn't laughing though, rather he was relieved a difficult time was over. The relationship with Port Vale was never repaired - some years later Jane remembers hearing from a Telford company telling them Graham had just over £500 in an account from pension contributions, they just needed pay slips from Port Vale to release the money: 'They wouldn't release any record of his wages...I think it could still be there - the company wouldn't even put the money into a charity.' Jane visibly shudders when talking about the time at Port Vale - whilst fiercely loyal to her husband and family at all times, she knows that Graham was not treated fairly and the impact of that was to cut short his playing career as well as cause significant financial distress. Jane remembers Woore friends' children asking their parents: 'Why don't the Hawkinses have any money?'.

Jane and Graham endured their own Winter of Discontent at Christmas 1979 - with no money for Christmas presents for the boys, Jane remembers: 'Christmas 1979 was different, we had Christmas Day with my Mum and Dad, calling to see Graham's Dad and Ann on the way. Mum and Dad made the day special and spoilt the boys, which was the important thing for both of us. We cashed in the insurance policies we had which really were not very much but we survived and promised the boys new bikes in the summer.' Richard and Ian had no recollection that Christmas 1979 was any different to any others - as far as they were concerned, unlike the bin-men, Santa Claus had not gone on strike.

After Port Vale, apart from the occasional game with the Shrewsbury Town Reserves, Graham wouldn't play professional football again. He made 67 appearances for Port Vale over a season and a half and was fit to play - it must have been devastating to end his playing career in this way. His Dad's retirement from Garrington's had been marked with a thank-you cheque - like most of Ernie's generation, a job was for life - instead of a thank you for his professional service to the game, Graham was facing the stress of negotiating a legal process and worries about how the mortgage was going to be paid. 'It just wouldn't happen today,' says Richard, 'The PFA have made sure no manager or player is sacked without compensation - they now have a large in-house legal team to support players.' Football circles are small now, but even smaller back in the late seventies, with very few overseas players and managers, reputation was everything. Despite being new to coaching, in 1979 Graham had 15 years' playing experience under his belt, and was well-known and respected by his peers and bosses for his professionalism and diligence. Ultimately, despite this early set-back, Graham would go on to enjoy a lengthy and rewarding career in football.

In the immediate aftermath of leaving Port Vale, Graham was hopeful of playing again and continued to train to keep fit. Speaking to Clive Corbett, author of 'Out of Darkness' on Wolverhampton Wanderers, Graham talked about that time: 'I trained at Stoke with Alan Durban for a while before Howard Kendall offered me a coaching job at Blackburn. Although I was flattered, I had only recently moved and really didn't want to move again.' Graham and Jane didn't move, but Graham did take the job. Kendall was another manager who would pass through Blackburn (1979 - 1981), before taking a job in the top flight, achieving great success at First Division Everton (signing Andy Gray from Wolves when Graham was manager - more on that later). Kendall had played at Port Vale's close neighbour and rivals, Stoke City, 1977 - 1979, and moved in the same circles as Graham. Graham and Jane were happy and relieved to be back at Blackburn after the turbulence at Port Vale - Graham enjoyed coaching 'a good bunch of lads', although after spending months commuting from Lytham to Burslem before the move to Woore was finalised, Graham was doing a similar commute in reverse. Jane remembers: 'Howard Kendall was a great character and we did see quite a lot of him, especially when he moved to Blackburn. He and Joe Mercer became strong friends and ended many a night with Howard's favourite tipple, champagne. He also spent time with Joe at Four Ways, St. Minver.' Graham's good friend Faz remembers Kendall asking about Graham, when he was considering taking him on as a coach, and talking in glowing terms about his friend and former team-mate.

Graham's full-time move into the coaching world involved attending as many games as possible, scouting out new players, checking out future opposition as well as networking with the football

A BRIEF FORAY INTO THE FOURTH DIVISION

world. Jane's diaries from that time reveal that Graham was hardly at home, and her life was equally busy, but parallel - a series of taxi-ing the boys around to their various activities (swimming, scouts, football, sleep-overs, cub camps), working at the school, coffee mornings, charity events, cleaning, cooking, shopping etc. In order to wind down after their busy days, she and Graham would sneak out for a drink at local pub the Coopers Arms, leaving the boys entertained by the TV. Jane and Graham became particularly close to the Coopers Arms' landlords Eric and Olwyn. With Graham often away from home, Jane would often pop in for some adult company, 'they'd never charge me, they were always so very kind.' The pub was close enough for the boys to walk there in the their pyjamas, or call if they needed Mum or Dad. Jane and Graham were good friends with all of their the neighbours, and knew they would help out if needed. Jane's diaries document the way the community worked together - Woore was a village well equipped to raise children.

After a few months at Blackburn, in January 1980 an opportunity came up at Port Vale's big rivals, Stoke City, coaching the U21s youth team. Alan Durban, who had tried to persuade Graham to go and play at Shrewsbury Town instead of taking the Port Vale role, had moved from Third Division Shrewsbury to manage Stoke in 1978, winning promotion to Division One in the last game of the season in 1979. Graham was happy coaching at Blackburn, but Stoke was so much closer to their new home and so he made the move to his fifth football club. Like Wolves, Blackburn and Preston, Stoke was one of the 12 founder members of the Football League - if Graham were playing EFL founding clubs bingo, he'd have at least a line. Their most famous player, Sir Stanley Matthews, was the first ever winner of the European Footballer of the Year (now known as the 'Ballon D'Or' - the Golden Ball) in 1956.

In the late seventies Stoke City played at the Victoria Ground, just off the A500, which was demolished and the ground developed as houses in 1997. At the time of its demise, it was the oldest operational ground in the Football League, Stoke's home since 1897. In 1976, a few years before Graham's brief time at Stoke, the roof of the stadium was blown off in a storm. Funding the repairs meant disposing of star players, including England goalkeeper Peter Shilton (to Nottingham Forest for £25,000) and forward Jimmy Greenhoff (to Manchester United for £120,000). With the loss of their star players, Stoke lost the relegation battle in 1977 and went down to Division Two, but when Graham started working there in 1980, they were in middle of their first season back in the top flight, having won promotion under Durban in 1979.

Jane remembers: 'Graham loved the youth team - young and enthusiastic. He and Alan got on well - he had known him for a while, just being on the footy circuit.' Graham described his time there to Clive Corbett: 'I was there for six months with Alan and it was really good working with the likes of Adrian Heath[10] and Lee Chapman[11] in the youth team.' Graham would have the satisfaction of seeing Lee Chapman carve out his first team career as a 20 year old, scoring his first goal for Stoke on 10 February 1980 in a 1-0 away win against Terry Venables' Crystal Palace. Teenager Adrian Heath also regularly appeared for the first team, scoring five goals in that 1979/80 season. During Graham's time at the helm at Molineux in 1983, there were press reports of Wolves taking an unhappy Lee Chapman from Arsenal, but without the funds to buy him, Graham could only offer a loan period, which was duly rejected by both player and club. Graham only worked briefly at Stoke, but he and Jane gained lifelong friends through the club. Well worth checking out is the 2014 BBC film 'Marvellous', which charted the heart-warming story of Neil Baldwin, lifelong Stoke fan with learning disabilities. His love of football and Stoke City perfectly illustrate how barriers can be transcended by the beautiful game. Jane often sees Neil with former Stoke players, on her 'WAG' walks around Trentham Gardens.

Whilst Graham was happy in his role at Stoke, ultimately he was looking to progress towards the top job. Graham was well-connected and well-respected in the football world, but his next job as assistant manager to Graham Turner at Alan Durban's old club, Shrewsbury, came through a more traditional route - he answered an advert in a newspaper and attended an interview. He'd been alerted to the opportunity on 20th June 1980, when the local paper reported that Reg Matthewson, Turner's assistant, had left his job to go and take a job at a chemical plant in Ellesmere Port. The next day, the advert appeared inviting applicants for the vacant post and Graham put pen to paper. Mr Matthewson's love of chemistry over football would prove a fortuitous move for Graham.

Shrewsbury were in Division Two in 1980. They had been promoted as Division Three champions under player-manager Turner in 1979. A relatively 'new' club, having joined the Football League in 1950, their time under Turner was to prove their golden era, with many 'giant-killer' moments. Graham's interview was a success, the job was his, and Graham's new commute would take him south-west to the fabulously named Gay Meadow. The start of the new decade meant that the difficult times of 1979 and Port Vale were behind Jane and Graham. Britain had a new prime minister, its first ever woman in the top job, Margaret Thatcher. Thatcher was unarguably ultimately a divisive leader, but she nonetheless heralded a new era. The strike-hit seventies felt shrouded in brown and grey hues, whereas the eighties were a shiny, fluorescent celebration of capitalism with new exciting gadgets appearing regularly, from microwaves, to video recorders, to space invaders. The Hawkins' boys Ian and Richard would enjoy the plethora of new toys that advances in technology made possible - Richard has fond memories of his bright yellow Sony Walkman - but it was a tough decade for the world of football. Fans deserted the terraces as other forms of entertainment became more widely available in an era before the advent of the big money TV deals of the nineties. Football clubs were dependant on gate receipts for revenue, and this was particularly challenging for smaller clubs like Shrewsbury Town. The growth of hooliganism on the terraces deterred many families from attending games and high levels of unemployment meant regular attendance was no longer affordable for the traditional working class supporter. The England team nonetheless qualified for the World Cup in 1982 - for the first time in 12 years - and English team Liverpool won the European Cup twice in the eighties, dominating the football scene both nationally and on the international stage, inspiring young Richard to support them (ssh - don't tell anyone at Carrington). Shrewsbury Town were some way off the pace of top flight football, but Graham's time there would prove to be a stepping-stone to a job he thought he could only dream of.

Graham at Port Vale. Thanks to the Stoke Sentinel for kindly allowing use of the image.

6 A Gay Time at the Meadow

1980 – 1982

Graham would spend two years under the tutelage of Graham Turner at Shrewsbury Town, affectionately known by Graham and his family as 'GT'. In the circle of life that is football, GT is the man who would pick up the Wolves job in 1986, two years after Graham's departure. Graham had a great deal of respect for GT, a player-manager who led by example. Talking to Clive Corbett, our Graham spoke fondly of his former boss, giving an insight to the job at hand: 'Graham was great to work with, there was no question of who the boss was but he let you get on with it. Two hard seasons went by, but we survived. The second season we had a real struggle at the bottom, but the chairman was wonderful. He told us that our jobs were under no pressure, to just get on with it and see what we could do. We survived and that is no mean feat.' Shrewsbury's gates were small compared to the rest of Division Two, leaving the manager the job of getting the best out of players without the money to spend big. Games were increasingly shown on TV, but gate receipts remained football's main source of income, with fixtures at bigger clubs drawing bigger crowds. The team had some success at home against Division One teams in cup games, requiring replays which helped the club's revenues.

Jane enjoyed taking the boys to watch Shrewsbury play at Gay Meadow in the town centre, recalling: 'Shrewsbury was a very happy time, a small club and everyone knew everyone. In the Blue Room after the game, we had sandwiches and cakes, made by the ladies on the staff.' Jane also had a role to play in the fortunes of the team: 'I can't really remember how it came about but one Friday I made couple of cheesecakes (out of a packet) requested by Graham to take for players after training. They won the next day so it became a regular thing for many home games.' Jane would enjoy browsing the shops on the way to the ground after parking up, although this did not impress Ian and Richard who would grab an arm each to frog-march her past Dorothy Perkins and the such-like. The boys remember times spent watching Shrewsbury Town, in particular ball-boy Fred Davies. There was only room for four men in the dug-out (manager, assistant manager, physio and 12th man), so Fred took up his position, cigarette in hand, just next to the dug-out, running off to find his coracle (rowing boat) on the river Severn, to collect the many stray balls that were booted out of the stadium. The stadium was demolished in 2007, problems with flooding meant many a cancelled game in inclement weather, lost revenue the club could ill-afford, and Shrewsbury Town moved to a new home, 'New Meadow'. Fred's coracle now has pride of place in the National Football Museum in Manchester.

Shortly after Graham took up his post at Shrewsbury Town, Lytham friends and neighbours, Chris and Dave, together with sons Gavin and Andrew came to visit Woore over the weekend of 25th August 1980. Their visit coincided with Shrewsbury Town's second home game of the season, a league match against Chelsea. The home team took a point off the London visitors in a 2-2 draw. However, the day was memorable for Richard, Ian and their friends for the hours spent giggling with a cassette player, recording commentary of the match that featured Chelsea defender John Bumstead. My two sons are both Bumsteads, a fact that brought this memory flooding back for my husband when we met in 2015. A few days later, Jane's diaries record that Richard and Ian went along to a golf testimonial organised for Graham's Blackburn team-mate and friend, Faz. The event was organised by Blackburn to mark his ten years at the club. The boys met a number of the Manchester United players, one of the perks of growing up in a footballing family, although as a Liverpool fan at the time, the event clearly did not impress Richard as he can't remember it.

Shrewsbury finished in 14th place in Division Two at the end of the 1980/81 season on 39 points, just three points ahead of

Graham's old team Preston North End, who were relegated along with Bristol City and Bristol Rovers. Surviving meant tight margins - the teams were still only getting two points for a win and one for a draw. That changed in the 1981/82 season, with the introduction of three points for a win, the brainchild of then Match of the Day presenter and chairman of Coventry City FC, Jimmy Hill. Hill believed that the introduction of three points for a win would discourage teams from settling for a draw, and thus create more exciting games for the fans. The change wasn't made in Europe for many years, with UEFA adopting the new scoring system only in 1995, but it is one that has stuck. Surviving the drop was a job well done for the two Grahams, and the Hawkins family went off for a well-earned summer break with their Blackburn friends in St Minver, Cornwall.

It was at family club Shrewsbury, that Jane and her boys would have their first serious encounter with football hooliganism, whilst tucking into tea and cake. After losing 1-0 in September 1981, disgruntled Chelsea fans lobbed a brick through the window of the 'Blue Room' as they trooped out of the ground. The Chelsea fans were amongst the most notorious, and violent confrontations with opposing fans became part of life for certain clubs throughout the eighties and nineties, documented in brutal fashion in the 2004 film, 'The Football Factory', starring Danny Dyer as a Chelsea fan unable to break away from the thrill of violent mobs. Chelsea didn't only bring hooligans to Gay Meadow though - A-list athlete Sebastian Coe also came to watch Chelsea lose at Gay Meadow, causing great excitement for sports fans Ian and Richard. Coe's support of Chelsea was news to me, a Sheffield girl, and if I'd have known this of the Sheffield-born athlete whilst watching him win gold in the 1980 Olympics, I'd have rooted for his rival Ovett.

Nigel Pearson[12] manager of Premier League clubs such as Watford and Leicester and former Sheffield Wednesday superstar, joined Shrewsbury Town as an 18 year old in November 1981, although he went on to make his senior debut after Graham had left, in 1982. Pearson appreciated Graham's coaching skills: 'I learned an awful lot, picking up good habits from the senior players I was playing with and the coaches,' Pearson said in 2014. 'If you have good role models around you – and we had lots of good senior pros – it gives you a good education. For a club of our size, with a squad of only 16 or 17 players, it was a great experience.' Pearson was Assistant Manager to Bryan Robson at West Brom when Richard joined as Head of Fitness and Conditioning, and Richard set up a call for me so I could ask him about his memories of Graham. Pearson told me about his football education at Shrewsbury Town, and that the values that Graham and indeed all of the club instilled in him, stayed with him throughout his career and still inform his managerial style today: 'I learned how coaches engaged with players to create good habits, learning behaviours so they can take care of themselves. Practice makes permanent, we were taught. At Shrewsbury we understood what we were and we worked at it to get that competitive edge.' He says of our Graham, 'He had a big effect on me. I couldn't have picked a better place to learn my trade. I came in as a wet-behind the ears teenager who needed toughening up. We did extra training in the afternoons on tennis courts and Graham would drive us there, in his Maxi. I remember, it was an automatic, a purple, maroon car. Graham just wanted to toughen me up and he'd push me into the fences. One time I leant into him and pushed him back. He'd then drive us back and I remember sitting there, not knowing what to say, feeling a bit uncomfortable about the whole thing.' Pearson stayed at Shrewsbury until October 1987, when he was bought by Sheffield Wednesday for £250,000, bringing much needed funds to the West Country club. Sheffield Wednesday were flying high in the First Division at the time, but Pearson remembers he wasn't phased, well-prepared by the team at Shrewsbury to deal with anything in the football world.

Shrewsbury Town were a small club in a small town, and in an environment of declining football gates across the country, needed a clear strategy for survival. Spotting young talent, coaching that young talent and then selling on to bigger clubs at a large profit was one way of making money. Surviving in Division Two was enough - they knew they didn't have the funds to make a go of it in the top tier, and so it made sense to move on any players who were good enough for Division One. Pearson was one such product of this strategy. Others included Paul Maguire, sold in the summer of 1980, just as Graham arrived, for £262,000 to former manager Alan Durban's Stoke. Ian

Atkins, another player destined for Division One, was sold at the end of our Graham's time at Shrewsbury in the summer of 1982 also to Alan Durban, then at Sunderland. Ian Atkins talked of the culture of Shrewsbury Town in the eighties to the Shropshire Star: 'Alan Durban brought the team together, Richie Barker gave it steel, determination and organisation. Graham Turner just carried it on. Sometimes managers come in and rip the thing to pieces. Graham didn't, he came in and just let it go, played himself and everybody moved on. It was just a great era to play in.' Pearson remembers how different football was back then: 'We were like a band of brothers. We survived every year on our home form. We got a cheque every two weeks that we'd all queue up to cash at Lloyds bank. We worked hard and played hard. Pre-season we used to go running in the Shropshire hills, these incredible runs and then we'd go down into town, to the Crown on the corner. The directors would be in there and say, "well done, you've worked hard this morning lads, have a pint of shandy." On a Friday after training we'd go into town and get a coffee. I remember one Friday it was snowing hard, and we were playing Chelsea the next day in The FA Cup. We all went to the ground to help clear the pitch along with a few fans who'd also turned up. We understood how important it was to get the game on so the club could get the match-day takings.'

Graham's second season at Shrewsbury was again about surviving in Division Two, although there was excitement to be had with some success in cup runs. Shrewsbury Town memorably beat UEFA-Cup holders Ipswich Town in the fifth round of The FA Cup, the Grahams beating the future England manager, Bobby Robson. The sixth round match, an away fixture at Leicester City on 5 March 1982, saw Shrewsbury sunk 5-2. An eventful game - Shrewsbury took the lead at 2-1 and then the Leicester goalkeeper went off injured. At a time when teams were still only allowed one substitute, typically an outfield player, this was a major loss to the home side. An unfortunate back pass led to an own goal that put Leicester level, and the magic of a 21-year old Gary Lineker in securing the win for Leicester did not go unnoticed by our Graham. Shrewsbury finished 18th in Division Two in 1982, two points off the drop zone - they had survived yet again, winning 11 matches, the same as the previous season.

The Grahams were back at Shrewsbury Town in pre-season training in the summer of 1982, when our Graham got a call out of the blue from Derek Dougan with an unexpected job offer. Both David Tossell[13] and David Harrison[14] interviewed Graham as part of their 2008 biographies on Dougan after his sudden death from a heart attack, and Graham recalled the moment Dougan got in touch with him out of the blue, 15 years after Graham had left Wolves: 'I hadn't followed any of what was going on at Molineux when Derek got in touch with me. I hadn't spoken to him for such a long time and wondered what he wanted me for. We were old team mates and I shared a room with him when we went out to America to play as the Los Angeles Wolves. I think I was the only player who was prepared to put up with all of his talking. Anyway, when he rang me, he asked me if I wanted to go and work for him, I said, "Where and what as?" I honestly didn't know he had taken over at Wolves. When he told me he wanted me as his manager, it was quite a shock. The answer was obviously "yes". I was thrilled and honoured. I was full of pride for myself and my family who all grew up as Wolves fans. They had always been my team. I had stood and watched them on the South Bank when I would be one of the first through the turnstiles every Saturday.' Graham told Tossell, 'I don't even know how he got my number.'

There had been speculation in the press about Graham becoming the new manager of Wolves, but not our Graham, rather there were whispers of Graham Turner being offered the job. Upon discovering that Graham Hawkins had been appointed, many were asking who he was. I wondered whether it was the fault of Ernie Hunt and Mike Bailey for their columns in the Sports Argus in the sixties, writing about their old pal 'Harry' Hawkins! Not that it concerned Graham in the slightest, 'When the newspaper headlines came out next day asking, "Graham Who?" it didn't bother me. I wasn't the best paid manager in the game and didn't even negotiate a bonus for winning promotion. That didn't concern me either. I was just delighted to be given the job. All I asked was would I be able to get on with the job without any interference from Derek or anyone else.' Funnily enough, the story that the job was going to Graham Turner originated from the one journalist Graham went on to trust and a man who became a good friend during the Hawkins reign at Molineux. Ironically, David

A GAY TIME AT THE MEADOW

Harrison of the Wolverhampton Express and Star did know who our Graham was, having watched him play for Wolves as a 12 year old from the South Stand, remembering Graham's shock of blonde hair as reminiscent of some great Wolves players including Billy Wright and Ron Flowers. As a young reporter, Harrison was at the ground when he heard that Dougan was off to Shrewsbury to meet Graham and thinking he'd got a scoop, broke the story of Graham Turner's appointment the next day. Harrison told me: 'I had a dollop of egg on my face because I'd got the story wrong,' and he set about making amends, knowing that it would be important to build a relationship with our Graham. He won Graham's trust early on: 'He told me he was after player such and such, but that I couldn't use it. I didn't use the story and a few days later I asked Graham how he was getting on and he told me that he wasn't interested in that player, that he'd just tested me out. After that he shared everything and we became pals.'

Whilst Dougan did not interfere with Graham's management of the team at Wolves, he is nonetheless the reason why Graham got the top job. A very different character to Graham, the two men maintained a mutual respect for each other, possibly acknowledging quiet, diligent Graham was a good foil to Dougan the showman. Whilst unproven as a first team manager, our Graham's appointment made perfect sense to Dougan. He was a Wolves man, he was a captain and he had spent much of his career in Division Two. Newly relegated, Wolves needed a manager who understood the teams in the second tier and who didn't expect big money signings. Dougan was a bit of a wanderer and had failed to settle at any club until he arrived at Wolves. The fans loved him and he loved them. Dougan knew Graham was the right man at the right time.

When Graham left Wolves in January 1968, the then 26 year old Dougan was cementing his place in the fans' hearts as well as the club's spot in Division One - top scorer in both the 1967/68 and 1968/69 seasons. He went on to play for Wolves for eight years, making 323 appearances and scoring 123 goals. Up until his time at Wolves, Dougan had not stayed anywhere very long; other than the four years he'd spent as a teenager in his home-town club, Belfast Distillery, his time at his other clubs, including Blackburn, was limited to a maximum of two full seasons. Irrepressible, if he disagreed with the manager and saw a better way, he was fearless in expressing his views, which was not always welcomed by those in charge. Passionate and belligerent about causes he believed in, Dougan was a force to be reckoned with. In 1970 he became chairman of the PFA and campaigned for the freedom of players to leave clubs at the end of their contract, reaching a deal in 1978. Dougan had a lot to say, writing 11 books before his death in 2008, including the 1981 opinion piece, confidently entitled: 'How Not to Run Football', as well as excelling at TV and radio football punditry. A Northern Ireland international who played alongside George Best, Dougan forged a friendly game of a united Irish team in 1973 against the then champions of the world, Brazil. An event that took place in the centre of a political furnace, with violence erupting in the Troubles that would last around 40 years until the Good Friday agreement of 1998, Dougan's international career for Northern Ireland ceased thereafter. Derek Dougan was a man who shot from the hip, passionate, charming and more than comfortable with using his position in the spotlight to make his points.

After leaving Wolves aged 34, Dougan became player-manager at Kettering Town, but football management was not where he wanted to be, he wanted to be running the show, making the strategic decisions, so he appointed ex-Wolves youth player Brian Thompson to manage the team. He negotiated the first ever shirt sponsorship deal with Kettering Tyres, much to the annoyance of The FA who demanded the shirts not be worn, claiming the deal went against FA rules. Fast forward to 4th August 1982, the day of heir to the throne, Prince William's christening, Dougan had been in role as chief executive of Wolverhampton Wanderers for a matter of days before Graham Hawkins was unveiled as the new manager.

Wolves stayed in the First Division for ten years after their 1967 promotion, dropping into Division Two for just one season in 1976/77. It would be the only time that Graham would face Wolves on the opposing team, playing in both league matches for Blackburn, winning the away game at Wolves in November 1976, but losing the return fixture at Blackburn in April 1977, when Wolves were well on their way to bouncing back up to Division One as Division Two champions. In the summer of 1982, Graham would have been aware that Wolves had once again been relegated, and would have contemplated returning to his old stomping ground with Shrewsbury Town in the coming season, but was not following the press on Dougan's involvement as a bidder to rescue Wolves from the financial quagmire that was on the verge of sinking the club forever. At a cost of £2.3 million, in 1979 Wolves had opened their new John Ireland stand (now the Steve Bull Stand) at Molineux, borrowing heavily from Lloyds Bank and the board was divided about how to deal with the crippling debt. The United Kingdom was gripped by recession in the early eighties, and in the summer of 1982, interest rates had surged to over 20%. Declining gates as a result of financial hardship plus the ever-increasing interest cost was pushing Wolves over the edge. Furthermore, having just been relegated, the mood in the dressing room was low. Something had to be done, and a number of options were being considered, namely selling star player Andy Gray to raise funds and/or selling land owned by the club and developing a supermarket on it. Selling players would bring in much needed funds quickly, but would anger already frustrated fans at a time when gate receipts were the club's financial lifeline. Any property development plans would take time the club didn't have to bring in the funds needed to stabilise the club.

Things at Wolves came to a head in June 1982, when the incumbent chairman, Harry Marshall, resigned after pressure from a number of other shareholders, including Doug Ellis, former Aston Villa chairman, who then replaced Marshall as chairman. Doug Ellis called in the administrators on 2nd July, accountants Peat Marwick in Birmingham, and they went about seeking a buyer to rescue the club from oblivion. The deadline for final bids was given as 30 July 1982, less than four weeks away, and the race started to raise the funds to take control of the club. Favourites to win in the press were new chairman Doug Ellis and his partner, Malcolm Finlayson a former Wolves goalkeeper: their bid amounted to £1.8m. Also in the running was Ken Wheldon, chairman of Walsall FC, with the backing of Sir Jack Hayward[15], local businessman whose bid of £1.65m was unsuccessful in 1982.

A MARRIAGE MADE IN FOOTBALL

Shareholders Roger Hipkiss and Doug Hope joined forces with Dougan to launch their own bid for the club. Hope, a lifelong Wolves fan and local businessman had befriended Dougan through the club and Hope believed Dougan had the skills to run the football club, but they needed financial backers. Hope got in touch with a company called Allied Properties through a mutual connection, and a meeting in a Portakabin in Manchester Airport with their senior management and shareholders of Allied Properties, the Bhatti brothers, sealed the deal. The two Bhatti brothers, a secretive pair, turned up to that fateful meeting wearing full Arab dress, convincing Dougan and his partners Hipkiss and Hope, that they had connections to the Saudi Arabian royal family and on the face of it, funds that Wolves so desperately needed. Dougan, a consummate and persuasive speaker, convinced Allied Properties of his credentials to run the football club and their backers were happy there was a property deal to be done. The property deal hung on getting planning permission from Wolverhampton Council for the supermarket, and Hope, having spoken to the council leaders, believed they would be supportive.

In April 1982 Argentina had invaded some islands off their southerly coast, known to them as 'Las Malvinas', a move that would trigger the 10 week-long Falklands War. Britain's victory would be a turning point for the popularity of the new prime minister, Margaret Thatcher, securing her victory in the general election in 1983. News of Britain at war and its aftermath would dominate the front pages for every day henceforth, although in David Harrison and Steve Gordo's book on 'The Doog', Hope recalls the attention given to his bid to save the Wolves gave rise to some difficult questions at home: 'we even replaced the Falklands War as the main item on some news bulletins. I remember getting home late one night and my then wife Shirley asked me who was this "millionaire property developer Doug Hope"?'

The Dougan bid was successful and on 31 July 1982, just 28 days away from the first match of the 1982/83 season, a home game against Graham's old club Blackburn Rovers, Dougan set to work on the rebuild of Wolverhampton Wanderers. Graham told the story to Clive Corbett, related in his book: 'Out of Darkness - History of Wolves 1977 - 90': 'After I pinched myself I can remember asking who was going to pick the team and be in charge of the coaching. To both questions he retorted, "You are". I got his assurance that he would not interfere in anything and that was the stipulation since I didn't want any interference whatsoever. I said, "If I'm going to manage, I'm going to manage. I'm not going to be a yes man to you." Ironically, I had just applied for a job as manager at Wrexham. I went in to see Graham and he was fine. It was never about money, although I was offered £20,000 a year. After my first pay packet I went out and bought a video so that I could watch games.'

    Richard remembers his Mum and Dad gathering the family in the kitchen to tell them the exciting news and swear them to secrecy. Richard recalled: 'I just remember thinking my friends at school would be impressed!' Jane describes how Graham took the news: 'Graham never made spur of the moment decisions and would always think things through, so he kept it all secret until he had talked it over with Derek and it was certain. Once the decision was made, we told the boys and family and then it was on Teletext[16] and the news. All the family were really thrilled. Graham just wished his Mum had been there to share the excitement.' I asked Graham's brother Andrew how he found out about Graham's new job: 'That was a massive shock lol. The build up was all top secret. I didn't even know he had applied for the job. My Dad knew but was sworn to secrecy. I remember it like it was yesterday, I hadn't long started seeing Gail and I spent a lot of time at her Mom and Dad's and Gail's brother also lived there - he was a massive Wolves fan. It was 10pm on the night and we were waiting for it to be announced on ITV News at Ten who the new manager was going to be. I was sitting one end of the settee, Gail was in the middle and her brother Martin at the other end, then the presenter said "we can now announce the next manager of Wolverhampton Wanderers". Myself and Martin at this point were sitting on the edge of our seats, then he announced "the new manager is Graham Hawkins" then up popped a picture of him on TV. We both froze, turned to each other with mouths wide open in disbelief. Shocked would be an understatement. I felt numb but excited and proud if that makes sense.'

Graham's first post as manager was to be at one of the biggest clubs in the country, a founding member of the Football League. They had just been relegated to Division Two, but the expectation of the fans and the football community was that this was a top flight team. The team counted Andy Gray in the squad, the UK's most expensive footballer when Wolves signed him in September 1979 for just under £1.5m. Jane remembers that none of this worried Graham, 'Graham was totally confident about his ability and nothing really phased him.' Graham told Clive Corbett: 'I've reflected on it since, but nobody has been in the position I was in. I've been a fan, apprentice, player and manager.'

Ian Greaves was an experienced manager, and some in the press were scathing of his sacking, but Dougan felt it was important that the takeover at Wolves should represent a changing of the guard. He told the press: 'I am thrilled and delighted that for the first time since Stan Cullis we have a Wolves man as manager at Molineux. I would like to think he knows this division like his two hands. It is an unknown territory for us and I believe Graham's knowledge will be a tremendous plus factor. Whatever he says and does he does so in his own right and in his own way. If Graham wants a player we will sit down with Stewart Ross[17], our financial advisor, and look at our state of affairs. Likewise, no player will leave this club unless the manager says so, not Derek Dougan.'

Jane was grateful not to be moving house, a little sad that the two years at Shrewsbury were over, but overall, the family were excited about the opportunity: 'Leaving Shrewsbury Town was hard as we had had such a lovely time there. Move on time, that's football and we knew it was going to be very different and difficult, but it was what Graham wanted to do. The fact that they were so close to folding and the Doog and consortium saved Wolves in the final minutes all added to the amazing situation.'

A GAY TIME AT THE MEADOW

WELDON,
BLUNTINGTON HOUSE,
CHADDESLEY CORBETT,
NR. KIDDERMINSTER,
DY10 4NR WORCS.
CHADDESLEY CORBETT 283

3/5/83.

Dear Graham,

Well done.

Sincerely,

Stan Cullis.

---

26 May 1983

TELEMESSAGE LXP   GREETINGS-B
THE MANAGER
WOLVERHAMPTON WANDERS FOOTBALL CLUB
THE MOLINEUX GROUND
WOLVERHAMPTON

Many congratulations on reaching the First Division. Well done.

Bob Paisley
Liverpool Football Club

Two of the many telegrams and letters congratulating Graham on Wolves' promotion to the top flight. Recognition from his former boss Stan Cullis and beating Bob Paisley's Liverpool at Anfield were two career highlights.

7 A Game of Two Halves

1982-83 First Half

As soon as Graham's appointment as Wolves manager had been announced in the press on the fourth of August, work had to begin. Back at home in Woore, the phone didn't stop ringing with messages of congratulations and cards and telegrams poured in from well-wishers. Jane lovingly kept them all, putting them into three albums for posterity together with many clippings from the newspapers. Alongside messages from many fellow football managers, including Bob Paisley (manager of First Division Champions, Liverpool) and former England legend, ex-Wolves and Liverpool player, Emlyn Hughes (at the time, Division Two Rotherham United manager), sit letters from fans, family and friends as well as a sweet note from the best friend of Graham's sister Maureen, Dot Humpage and her husband Ernie. She writes to congratulate Graham and goes on to say: 'As soon as I knew of your appointment I phoned Maureen and she said she hadn't been able to speak to you since your appointment because she had not been able to catch you in. But as you can guess, she is delighted for you. I hope you don't mind me writing to you Graham; when I told Maureen she said you would probably be pleased that I should be interested enough to write to you.' Also included in the album, on Leicester University-headed note paper, is a note from school-friend and former team-mate David Siveter, 'I confess I fell off my chair with surprise (and delight!) when I read of the news, but I also have faith in Mr Dougan's choice! Had my Dad been alive he would have been as proud as you and your family on your appointment.' David goes on to tell Graham that he and his wife took up their place on the South Bank to cheer on Wolves at their first game of the season. Graham's new job had caused a great deal of excitement in many quarters.

A GAME OF TWO HALVES

Wolverhampton had nearly lost their prestigious football team, rescued from the brink by Dougan and the funding sourced by Allied Properties. Now for the first time since the end of the golden years of Stan Cullis, a local man was at the helm as manager. It might have been Graham's first job in charge, but he'd been in the game long enough to know he was up to it and had learned from a number of successful managers he'd worked with. He was also comfortable at Molineux, his home club. Come Graham's first day in the office, he needed a number two. Fortunately, Jim Barron was already in situ as former manager Ian Greaves' assistant. Graham had played with Barron from when he had been a goalkeeper in the early sixties at Wolves and the pair had got on well. Barron was an experienced goalkeeping coach and was respected by the players - Graham quickly decided he was the man for the job and the men became good friends. Barron was happy to talk to me about his time with Graham at Wolves and he recalled being particularly tickled by a Sunday Times article that described him and Graham as 'the Starsky and Hutch of the football league', with Graham's look as Robert Redford and Barron channelling Paul Newman. Another key support for Graham came from Frank Upton - appointed as youth coach early in that first season - a vital role given the reliance Graham would have to place on young players given the lack of funds for new talent.

The cash-strapped club didn't even have a physio, with players having to resort to sourcing their own treatment. Physio Denis Conyerd literally walked in off the street offering his services. Conyerd had his own sports injuries practice in Wolverhampton, but dreamed of one day working for his beloved football club. On Barron's recommendation, he was more than happy to share his stories with me, of the time he spent at Molineux, all in all working under six managers by the time he left in 1986. 'I used to go Wolves, since I was a nipper when they had 52,000 on the terraces,' Conyerd told me, going on to recall how he'd got his job back in 1982. A friend of his wife's had heard Dougan on local radio station, Beacon Radio, and called up Carol Conyerd to tell her, knowing how much her husband would have loved the job. 'My wife called me three times the next day, she forced me into it,' Conyerd recalled. His job interview was somewhat unorthodox and not quite what he expected: 'There I was, dressed up in a suit, hoping for a bit of coffee and a biscuit in the board room, but when I got there, Derek Dougan introduced me to Graham and said "right, follow me" and led me past the manager's office on the right and past the green room, where the directors used to have a drink with their wives, straight into the treatment room. Graham sat on the draining board. It was a four hour interview - there were seven players there waiting to be treated.'

Speaking to Conyerd, it's clear that he has a great deal of respect and fondness for Graham: 'I was new to football and Graham taught me how to behave in football, what to expect. Graham, Jim and Frank Upton they had this discipline you see, they were old school, they knew what discipline was. They had a good set-up, it was fun to go to work, all these jokes and vibes going on, it was a really good time.' Conyerd was on the receiving end of that discipline a couple of times in the early part of his time at Wolves, and recalls one occasion during a training session at Molineux when Graham was leading the warm-down of the players. Conyerd mistakenly thought he should share some of his medical knowledge on the best way to breathe from the diaphragm: 'Back in the changing room I got what you call nowadays the hairdryer treatment from Graham,' he recalled, '"Don't you ever interrupt my training session again," he said. "Learn your department and stay in it," that's what I took from that.'

Conyerd was incredibly proud to have played his part at Wolves with Graham and related the moment he got his official Wolves kit: 'It was the first pre-season game against Swindon. Jim Barron came up to me and said, "Hold your arms out" and he handed me everything, all the kit, shorts, socks, training shoes, everything. I got home and my wife was out at work and I put it all on and walked out and around the garden. I couldn't believe I was part of this set-up.'

Graham had less than a month to prepare the team for their first league game; at home against former club Blackburn Rovers. His only experienced goalkeeper, Paul Bradshaw, was injured and would be unable to start. His £1.5 million striker, Andy Gray, was injured and wanted to play First Division football, speaking openly of his desire to leave. The skeleton players and staff that were left had been beset with the uncertainty of the club's survival over the summer as well as the despondency of relegation. The club had been decimated. The new physio, Conyerd, brought in his own equipment to work, finding the club just didn't have the kit he needed.

Dougan and Graham had very different roles to play, but found they complemented each other well. Dougan was the front-man of Wolves, happy in the spotlight, innovative and unafraid of controversy. He went about his task with ruthless efficiency, firing commercial manager and former referee Jack Taylor as well as company secretary Phil Shaw in quick succession, putting in his own men, including Eric Woodward as general manager, formerly of Aston Villa. At the same time, he brought back some of the old faithful back office staff from the Cullis era, including the coach driver, Sid Kipping. Dougan also started a charm offensive on the fans, keen to restore that family feeling at Wolves to encourage supporters back into the ground on match days.

Graham spoke to David Harrison about his relationship with Dougan: 'Derek was fine to work for. He was very much a technical director and that was way ahead of his time. He never interfered. We would get together for a scotch on a Friday afternoon and I would tell him what my team was for the next day. He would ask me why I was doing this or that and questioned a selection here and there, but he never tried to get me to change things. He always supported me - unless he was doing things behind my back and I doubt that very much. He would come into the dressing room and have a chat with the players sometimes, but I didn't mind that because we were very much a family club. Derek wasn't a coach and he knew that, so all he wanted to do was give the lads a bit of extra motivation. He never put any pressure on me and in fact I think he kept a lot of pressure away from me.' Graham was much happier away from the spotlight, at the training ground, immersed in the day to day of coaching and managing a football team.

Given his background in the lower divisions of the football league, Graham knew he had to set his stall out early on in the dressing room, in order to gain the trust and respect of the senior players and he was unafraid to lay down the law. 'I'm looking for the right response from them all. If they play badly but give me 100%, that will be okay,' he reported at an early press conference. Fines for indiscretions such as arriving late at training, getting found in the pub in the lead up to a game and dissent on the pitch were established early and policed consistently, to such an extent that on one occasion Graham had to fine himself £70 for getting frustrated with the referee after a game against Fulham in January 1983. 'How can I preach to the players when I can't control myself?' Graham told the press at the time. Whilst Graham set the sanctions, he got the players to devise their own bonus scheme, telling the press in October 1982: 'They know that if they want bonuses, they have to keep winning and stay at the top. The players planned it that way, and it is such a nice feeling, knowing that such an idea came from them. They must stay in the top bracket if they want to earn their corn.'

Unsurprisingly for the times, Graham never received any formal press training, but he would invariably have to engage with journalists as part of the job. Jane remembers: 'Graham was naturally a quiet person but once on his subject could talk for ever. He was right in the deep end but coped with it.' Reading through the press from his time as Wolves manager, as well as quotes from interviews he gave to Clive Corbett, David Harrison and David Tossell, Graham comes across as open, honest and straight-forward about his team's performance, saving any criticism of individual players for behind closed doors. Jane's analysis of a quiet man, but happy to chat for hours about his area of expertise are traits I recognise all too well in my husband Richard.

There was a lot riding on Graham's first match - it would set the scene for the season ahead. The first crisis he needed to resolve was the lack of goalkeeper, and his solution in the form of John Burridge ('Budgie') would prove to be a shrewd move. Burridge was at Terry Venables' QPR, but keen for a move to get away from their controversial artificial pitch. His first outing wasn't reassuring though; Graham described it to Clive Corbett: 'It was in a practice match against Coventry at Castlecroft. His gloves and kit were pristine, everything was just right. I watched from the little stand where twenty years earlier Stan Cullis had watched me and told me to use my right foot more. Five to ten minutes in a cross came over, Budgie came out to get it and missed it completely. We were one down. He was so keen and wanted a move, assuring me, "Don't worry boss, it'll be fine, it won't happen again." He was true to his word.' Not only did Burridge make some vital saves, particularly when Wolves were clinging on to their promotion spot in the final games of the 1982/83 season, but was an inspirational character in the dressing room to an exceptionally young and inexperienced squad. Always joking, performing handstands as part of his showman-like warm-up to entertain the crowds before a game, his commitment to training was second to none.

In David Harrison and Steve Gordos' book on Dougan, they had no doubt about the challenges ahead: 'Hawkins faced the most difficult task of all. He had to assemble a squad in time for the season's kick-off against Blackburn Rovers on 28 August. He had very little to work with apart from disillusioned seasoned professionals like Andy Gray and Joe Gallagher, loyal stalwarts like Mel Eves, Wayne Clarke and Geoff Palmer and a bunch of enthusiastic, but totally untried and untested youngsters. If saving the club was a miracle, the job Hawkins did in steering Wolves to promotion that season was more akin to discovering the Holy Grail and the meaning of life put together. It is an achievement often forgotten in the history of the club. He began by putting out a team on the opening day which included four teenage debutants, Ian Cartwright, Paul Butler, Billy Livingstone and David Wintersgill, who was a 16 year old straight from school.' Incidentally, Wayne Clarke was another local boy, the youngest of five footballing Clarke brothers, some 15 years the junior of Graham's contemporary from his Darlaston days, Allan.

Anyone in football will tell you that luck always plays a part, and Wolves' first fixture against Graham's former club, about which he knew so much, was a blessing. At half-time, Wolves were losing 1-0, but they ended up winning the game. Graham shared some insights into his management style to Clive Corbett: 'Against Blackburn we should have been seven down at half-time, not one, we got battered. It was important that my half-time talk did not deflate them. I was not a dressing room ranter and raver. I knew that their full backs didn't like to head the ball, particularly their left-back. We had to get balls to the back post. Paul Butler gets on, two balls to the back post, bang, bang, 2-1. All of a sudden it's changed, all of a sudden this fella knows what he's talking about, I've proved myself.'

Jane went to every home game, supporting her husband come rain or shine, win or lose. The family would drive down to Wolverhampton on Saturday morning, dropping Graham off then going back to see Jane's parents, returning to Molineux for the three o'clock kick-off. A couple of games in, once Graham was in his stride, Ian and Richard joined the Wolves family and took up positions as ball-boys, one each side of the dug-out. Jane remembers fun times: 'My Mum came with me to the games, which I loved, being as the boys were doing their ball boy thing. Mum really enjoyed being part of it all, special seats and a blanket to keep you warm on chilly days. Plus tea and cake at half-time.' Both Ian and Richard loved being ball boys, and took their responsibilities very seriously. Coached in reading the game, they were under strict instructions to get the ball back as quickly as possible if Wolves needed a goal, to take their time if they needed to see out the game. Richard recalls kicking the ball back onto the pitch for a free kick when Wolves needed to keep the game moving, the ball whistling a little too close to the head of an injured Viv Anderson, whose look revealed he was not impressed with the 12 year old in his old gold ('it's not yellow,' Jane corrected me in horror) and black tracksuit. Barron recalled how well trained young Richard and Ian were, playing their part in supporting the Wolves. Physio Conyerd also remembers being schooled in ball-boy best practice in the pre-season: 'We were in Belfast playing Glentorans and desperate to keep winning. With ten minutes to go, it was their throw in and the ball landed at my feet. I threw it to the opposition player and they got a quick throw-in, could have scored from it. Got my second hairdryer treatment after that from Jim and Graham.'

The winning start against Blackburn continued throughout September, and by mid-October, the Wolves were still unbeaten and top of the table. Always a little superstitious, Graham confessed to the press that he had worn the same suit to every match, and wouldn't change it until Wolves were beaten in the league. Unfortunately, he jinxed their run, losing 3-0 at home to Leicester on 16 October 1982, shortly after the interview, Gary Lineker scoring the second. The loss meant QPR knocked Wolves off the top spot. Having not conceded a league goal for 817 minutes, giving away three against local rivals hurt. At the following game, a league cup replay against old pal Alan Durban's Division One Sunderland, it seemed like the floodgates had opened as Wolves let in five. It was a prescient sign of the gulf in playing level between the top two divisions. Graham had played Andy Gray against Sunderland, taking out 17 year old Billy Livingstone who had been filling the gap whilst he was injured. Graham had seen the decision coming, praising the youngster in an interview at the beginning of October: 'I don't believe in dropping a player when they're doing well. There was a time when I couldn't imagine leaving a fit Gray out, but I may have to face such a decision soon.' It was a recurring dilemma Graham faced throughout his two years in charge of a squad that was severely lacking in depth - having to throw young, inexperienced players in the deep end, when he would have preferred to allow them to be more carefully introduced into the first team squad. Graham told Clive Corbett of the dilemmas caused by injuries and a lack of depth in the squad: 'We had a lot of seniors, no middle and then the youngsters. I didn't have to pick the teams at that time. They picked themselves. My only thought was: "How do I play these 11 players?" In the end, some of those boys ended up getting ruined because of the pressure they were under. But they had great attitudes and showed the older lads what could be achieved through skill and determination and then the older ones took over.' All the more important then, that on the back of successive 3-0 and 5-0 defeats, Graham was able to motivate and inspire his team to pick themselves up and go again.

Former players also commented on the positive changes that Dougan and Graham brought to Molineux at that time, including Kenny Hibbitt, captain in the 1983/84 season, persuaded to return from the US to join the new regime, shortly after the start of Graham's first season. Kenny told the press in January 1983: 'I have never been happier in my 14 years in the game. The players are on first name terms with the directors and everyone's relaxed. We were treated like serfs before…now we're treated like human beings.'

A MARRIAGE MADE IN FOOTBALL

Not everyone was happy, though, and November 1982 saw centre-half Joe Gallagher leave Wolves in a cloud of bad feeling. Disgruntled, Joe had made remarks in the press that he was only prepared to give 75%. Upon hearing this at two o'clock, Graham immediately dropped him from the team playing at three o'clock. When Gallagher subsequently refused to appear in the team photograph, Dougan acted decisively, tearing up his contract. Graham recalled: 'I got rid of Joe Gallagher. I didn't want him there, discipline-wise it was difficult. I said to Derek, "I've had enough, he's breached his contract".'

November's results were mixed, alternately winning and losing, unable to get on a run, but five games in December brought four wins and a draw. His success earned Graham the Division Two 'Manager of the Month' award complete with a gallon bottle of Bells whisky - an amazing achievement just four months into Graham's managerial career. The whisky bottle went on its own journey with Jane and Graham and, according to Jane: 'It did eventually get drunk, and we had a good return on it as it went on an optic and got bought by customers and given to friends when we were in the pub[18]. I remember Eric and Olwyn at the pub looked after it while we were in Bahrain[19], and the bottle was used after to save pound coins.'

Christmas is usually a busy period for all those who work in football, although the fixtures fell kindly in 1982, with an away game at Graham's old club Shrewsbury Town on 27th December instead of the usual Boxing Day, and for once the players and manager got a day off on Christmas Day. Jane remembers Christmas in Woore as a village affair: 'We all went for a drink on Christmas Day with our friends, the Porritts, and other neighbours to the Coopers Arms - it was a really lovely atmosphere. Kids with pressies and adults in an assortment of sweaters.'

The Wolves managed to continue their winning run against Shrewsbury Town, and were back on top of Division Two when rivals QPR lost to Chelsea, staying there after another win at home against Burnley. Wolves started the year three points clear at the top and unbeaten in six games. QPR remained on their heels, and a humiliating

5-0 loss against their nemesis Leicester at the end of February, put QPR level on points at the top of the table, a position they would keep until the end of the season. Wolves results were mixed thereafter, with Burridge saving points on many an occasion, including saving two penalties against Sheffield Wednesday to preserve a 1-0 lead. Three teams would win promotion to the First Division at the end of the season, and despite a decline in form towards the end of the season, Wolves had done enough to go up as runners-up, after a nervy 3-3 draw away at Charlton. Graham recalls the moment in Clive Corbett's book: 'I wouldn't swap promotion for anything, but the game at Charlton when we were three up at half-time, dearie me. I couldn't calculate whether we were up or not. I remember waiting for somebody's results to confirm that we'd done it. I stood in the television room watching the results. By the time I got to the dressing room they were already celebrating, the champagne had already been popped.'

The first home game after winning promotion was the last game of the season on 14 May 1983 against Arthur Cox's Newcastle United. The away leg had been played in December on Richard's 11th birthday and Wolves had earned a 1-1 draw against a side lacking their star player, Kevin Keegan, due to injury. Graham knew Arthur well as he had coached him when a player at Preston North End, and in the pre-match briefing back in December, Arthur had a few kind words to say about him: 'I know something, Graham had two or three very good attributes as a player, which will stand him in good stead as a manager. He is very genuine and very honest. He did well at Preston but now he has to prove himself as a manager.' Graham had more than proved himself as a manager - he had led Wolves back into the top flight of football in his first season as a manager.

Richard remembers that end of season match well - his Dad had been concerned that there would be a pitch invasion after the match and gave Richard and brother Ian strict instructions to get off the pitch as soon as the final whistle was blown, so they would avoid any trouble. Before the game, Player of the Year and consummate showman, John Burridge came out on the pitch to perform his warm-up in a Superman outfit. Acrobatics were a regular feature of his warm-up and the crowd loved it. In his autobiography, 'Budgie', Burridge tells the story that Newcastle players Kevin Keegan and Chris Waddle bet him he wouldn't play in his outfit, which was just too tempting an offer: 'When we got into the dressing room I told the manager, Graham Hawkins, that I was going to play in it and he got a bit upset about it. The linesman would always come in about 2.45pm to check the studs. There was no sponsorship in those days, so I didn't have any logo I had to display and I wasn't breaking any rules. So I asked the linesman, and he said he had no objections as long as I didn't clash with the other team. So I took off the cape, kept the tights and the blue top and taped a number one onto my back. I put a pair of proper shorts on top of my blue tights and I ran out, half-Superman, half Wolverhampton Wanderers goalie.' Graham reluctantly let his player have his moment. It wasn't the first time - Jane remembers the Christmas party where the players were split on whether the dress code should be black-tie or casual, so Burridge went top half dinner suit, bottom half tramp, much to everyone's amusement.

Winning promotion was exhilarating, and Express and Star reporter David Harrison told me of the great pride Graham felt at receiving a letter from his hero, Stan Cullis, congratulating him on the achievement. Harrison, along with Barron, experienced the ups and downs of Graham's first season in charge so closely that they nicknamed him the 'twelfth man'. These were good times for men in their prime and after a long day's work, the three of them would often meet in the wine bar opposite the Express and Star offices in Wolverhampton. Harrison is in no doubt with regards to Graham's achievement: 'That amazing season - Graham never got enough credit for it, for what he achieved with a patchwork of a team and a lot of young kids who'd never even played for the first team before.'

Graham enjoying a cuppa shortly before kick-off at Molineux. Photograph kindly provided by Denis Conyerd, Wolves physio.

1983 – 1984 Second Half

Graham and Jane were on a high; Graham's first season in charge had gone better than anyone could have dreamed. When one set of grumpy neighbours back in Woore complained ('again') about Ian and Richard playing football in the street ('as well as the other 16 children,' says Jane), it felt like the right time to look for a house with a bigger garden. Jane's brother David talked to me about other reasons why Jane and Graham were looking to move house; Graham was becoming a celebrity, and occasionally fans or the press would turn up outside the house. Graham wanted to protect his family from any uninvited visitors. In May 1983 Springbank came on the market, a bungalow with an enormous garden and stunning outlook that was just two miles down the road. It was also secluded and gated, providing privacy from any stalwart fans who came for a glimpse of their team's manager. Both Jane and Graham fell in love at first sight. Jane recalls: 'We couldn't find much we could afford, then one day driving home Graham noticed a new for sale sign, to be sold at auction. The place was empty as the lady had passed away, Graham took me down to look round the garden and I loved it from the beginning. Graham went to the estate agent and asked all about it. Apparently a builder was very interested and he was going to knock it down and build big. Can't compete against a builder. Graham went back with an offer and was so passionate about it that when the agent spoke to builder he replied: "if he wants it that much let him have it".' This was to be the dream family home - smaller than their house in Woore village, with just the one bathroom and a layout whereby Richard's bedroom would be accessed through big brother Ian's room - but with a stunning three quarters of an acre garden overlooking open countryside, perfect for the boys who spent every waking hour outside playing football. In order to secure the house, Graham and Jane needed a bridging loan as they still needed to sell their house on Westfields Rise. Unable to get funding from the bank, Wolves stepped in to help. Jane recalls: 'Graham asked Doog to have a look and he understood why we wanted to move. The Wolves directors then said that they would cover the bridging loan and a letter was kept at NatWest confirming that.' The house needed rewiring and Graham's Dad Ernie and little brother Andrew spent many days ripping wood chip wallpaper off the walls before they eventually moved in, renting out Westfields Rise which remained unsold.

No one was in any doubt that Graham had achieved wondrous things in his first season as Wolves manager, but equally, he and the experienced players were fully aware that in order to survive in Division One, the squad needed serious investment. Experienced player Kenny Hibbitt summed up the challenge in an interview a couple of months before the season ended: 'Graham Hawkins ...he has the respect of the players - that's the most important of all - and we have a bit of fun and laughter in training, but he's always pushing you. Graham has done well to put us on the way to promotion. I don't think anyone dreamed we'd be up there before the season started. But if we do go up, there's a lot to be done - that's when the real work starts. In the Second Division there are lots of youngsters still trying to make it, but in the First, there are internationals who really know the game.'

Graham came up with a list of players he wanted, at an estimated cost of £750k - £1m. Top of the list was Leicester's Gary Lineker. Doug Hope maintained in an interview with Fanzine Wolfwhistle that the deal was done with both Gary Lineker and Leicester, had only the money been forthcoming. Both the Leicester and Wolves teams had celebrated their promotion to Division One in a hotel in Majorca - coincidentally the same hotel - and reportedly Gary was open to the move. Barron was somewhat sceptical when I asked him about a 'done deal with Lineker' - perhaps Hope was engaging in wishful thinking around 'what could have been'. Others included 24 year old Mick McCarthy, then at Barnsley, ultimately signed by Manchester City and David Seaman, a goalkeeper at Peterborough United that Barron liked the look of. No one could deny that Graham had an eye for young talent. Whilst John Burridge had performed brilliantly that season, Graham had been warned by Burridge's former boss at QPR, Terry Venables, that his wage demands might be prohibitive once Wolves were in Division One. This proved to be a prophetic warning, but unfortunately Burridge was not the only one looking for a pay rise that wasn't forthcoming.

During his tenure at Wolves, Graham had just the one grievance with his boss Dougan - Tony Towner. After an eventful first season, the Hawkins family took a much-needed break to Greek resort, Halkidiki. With Graham out of the country, Derek went and signed the winger for £100,000 from Rotherham. Barron was also on holiday in Tenerife - the deal was struck by Dougan during the only week when both men were away. David Tossell recalls the story in his book on The Doog: '"It was the only thing Derek did that I didn't totally agree with," says Hawkins, "I was on holiday at the time. We had seen Tony play and he was on our list but I didn't agree with the way it was done. Another winger was a low priority for me. Derek thought he would be another Dave Wagstaffe".' Unfortunately, Tony Towner was not the answer. 'Lovely guy though, Tony Towner,' Richard remembers, having met him some years later, 'Though I guess he wasn't what we needed at the time.'

Pre-season 1984, Graham took the team to Sweden and twelfth man Harrison was more than happy to don a shirt and join in, even taking up his place on the bench for one friendly, 'I just wish I'd got a picture of it,' he laughed. Fully embedded in the inner circle, Harrison recalls the club doctor, Bill Tweddle, relaying a tale to Graham and Barron over breakfast in the hotel one day, whereby one the players had got into a scrap with a team-mate, hitting him over the head with a bottle. Harrison told me: 'Graham had been at a meeting with Jim Barron with some Swedish officials so wasn't there and said: "Turn my back for five minutes - wonder what would happen if the press found out!" then laughed realising I was sat at the table.' Still true to his much-loved friend, Harrison didn't want to spill the beans on which players were involved. From the inside, Harrison gave me his thoughts on why Graham was a great manager: 'Good rapport with the players, close but not too close, very professional, very strict.' Assistant manager Barron was equally complimentary, 'He gave the impression that he was easy-going, and he was most of the time, but when it needed it he could be firm and direct. He didn't pick on the kids and forget the seniors - which some did - he was equal and fair with all of them.'

A GAME OF TWO HALVES

The opening game, at home against 1983 League Champions, Liverpool, featuring the likes of world class players Kenny Dalgleish and Ian Rush, was a moment of great excitement and anticipation, albeit the press was full of stories of contract disputes and injuries in the Wolves camp. Miraculously, Wolves went ahead after just two minutes, the first goal scored in the league that season, with captain Geoff Palmer converting a penalty after Andy Gray was brought down in the penalty area. Unable to contain the onslaught from the Liverpool strikers in the second half, a 1-1 draw after an Ian Rush equaliser a minute into he second half, was a magnificent result against the best opposition. Unfortunately, the lack of funds to reward existing players and attract much-needed new players, meant it was mostly downhill thereafter.

It's probably fair to say that the Bhatti brothers' interest in Wolverhampton Wanderers was limited to making a return on a property deal for which the council denied planning permission, and other than a bit of an ego trip, they had little interest in the long-term future of the football club. Plans were drawn up for a £20m investment into the club and surrounding area, and a 3D model sat proudly at Molineux, even featuring on Match of the Day in September 1983, five games into the new season. At the beginning of Graham's second season, there was still hope that at some point funds may be forthcoming to enable Graham to buy the players he needed, but the resignation on 1st October 1983 of Mike Rowland, CEO of the Bhattis' company, Allied Properties, was an ominous sign. Planning permission was never granted, the Bhattis would never make a return on their investment in Wolves. Consequently the Bhattis interest in the football club died alongside their property project. As the football team failed to win week after week, the directors made fewer appearances at Molineux, even shifting board meetings to London to avoid the wrath of the fans. Roger Hipkiss would later say that perhaps Graham won promotion too soon, but for me, that kind of statement merely befuddles the real issue at Wolves - the club's financial backers had no real interest in investing and developing a successful football team and the failure to get planning permission meant the decline was inevitable. Barron remembers meeting the Bhattis and that their objective was never to win the league: 'They'd say, "make sure we finish in the middle of the table, make sure we stay in the division, keep us safe". And then, when we were in the top six, "let's keep us there". There were promises of coaching jobs in the Middle East over the summer if we could stay in the division.' Whilst I haven't seen the accounts from that period, I understand that the majority of the Bhattis' funding to buy Wolves came from a bank loan secured on the real estate of Molineux, and without planning permission, they just didn't have the means to provide the necessary investment to fund a top tier team.

The directors weren't the only ones deserting Molineux - fan numbers also dwindled, as was commonplace across grounds in the early eighties, in an era when televised live football was in its infancy. Dougan was all for the cameras, telling the press: 'This is what the public want. They are fed up with all the canned stuff[20],' and along with a majority of Division One clubs, voted to grant rights to allow live Sunday matches to be screened on ITV. After Tottenham Hotspur and Nottingham Forest along with eighties novelty act, Chaz and Dave, provided the entertainment for the first live televised football match since 1960, Wolves got their turn on 23rd October 1983, hosting local rivals Aston Villa with great fanfare. Sixties' band, Dave Dee, Dozy, Beaky, Mick and Titch, headlined the event, that is until a power cut ended their set prematurely. Those clubs opposed to televising live football, were justifiably worried about declining attendances, and the Wolves game drew just over 13,000 fans, of whom over 2,000 gained free entry in order to comply with Sunday trading laws of the time. After losing five matches on the bounce, and yet to secure a win in the new season, Graham and the team were keen to put on a performance and halt their slide to the bottom of the table. Despite only securing a 1-1 draw, Graham felt optimistic after the game, telling the press: 'That was as well as we've played this season. If we continue to apply ourselves like that, our first win is not too far away.' Unfortunately it didn't come two days later, when the team suffered a second humiliating defeat by Third Division Preston North End, managed by Graham's old Blackburn boss, Gordon Lee, knocking Wolves out of the League Cup. After the first leg, Lee had been shocked to see how little support that Wolves were getting from the terraces: 'I have a soft spot for them because I nearly became their manager and used to support them as a kid. The fans need to give them some encouragement, rather than getting at them.' Whilst Jane found it difficult to hear the fans' abuse, she still went to every home game without fail, supporting her husband through thick and thin. She remembers: 'I really enjoyed the whole atmosphere being part of it all. From my point of view it was not a lot different those two seasons, apart from the results. I used to spend the whole game with my fingers crossed.' David Instone, football reporter at the Wolverhampton Express and Star who took on reporting on Wolves after David Harrison left, told me that mostly the ire of the supporters was directed against the Bhatti brothers, rather than Wolves-men Dougan and Graham.

Four days after the Preston defeat, Wolves lost 3-0 away at Old Trafford against Ron Atkinson's Manchester United; two goals from Frank Stapleton and one from Richard's future boss at West Brom, Bryan Robson[21], and they slumped to the bottom of the table, where they would stay until the end of the season. November brought more pain, with a 5-0 loss against Nottingham Forest, prompting their manager Brian Clough to commiserate with Graham: 'From what I've seen of Graham Hawkins, he's doing a superb job with limited help. I feel very sorry for him because it's a job I wouldn't fancy.' Whilst inherently true, it should be said that Brian Clough was in the midst of a public spat with Dougan and his choice of words was certainly designed to rattle Graham's boss. Dougan had lambasted Clough for opposing televising live football, leading him to respond: 'If I were responsible for appointing someone to the position Dougan holds, I would certainly want someone who is better at the job.' One of the most controversial and outspoken football managers of all time, Jane remembers Graham contacting Clough to enquire about a player only to elicit a two word response ending in 'off' before the receiver was slammed down.

By October 1983, Graham knew that no money would be made available for players and a number were refusing to sign contracts, feeling they deserved First Division wages. Hope told David Harrison and Steve Gordos in their book about 'The Doog' how bad the financial situation was in Graham's second season: 'As things went from bad to worse I was on the phone constantly to Gordon Taylor at the PFA for help. On one occasion he lent us £20,000 to pay the players' wages on time.'

Whilst Jane and Graham didn't spend much time discussing the ins and outs of football - it was too important for Graham to leave his worries behind and enjoy the sanctuary of his family life - Jane remembers the disappointment and frustration her husband felt once it became clear he would not be supported with the necessary funds: 'Yes it was an awful realisation there was no cash to buy players, especially as he had spent a lot of time watching players up and down the country and putting names forward. The hour drive home during this period gave Graham the chance to get the anger out of his system.' By 11th November, Graham was forced to sell his most valuable player, Andy Gray, who went to Howard Kendall's Everton for £250,000. The following day saw Dougan give a press conference in support of his manager, but new chief executive of Allied Properties, John Starkey, did not bring much comfort that Graham or the team would be supported in their mission to survive in Division One, saying: 'When it comes to cash for buying players, however, Derek and Graham need to wheel and deal in the transfer market.' Barron recalls: 'we weren't a million miles short, but we were short,' but given the tight margins of football, over the course of a long season that lack of depth would seal the team's fate.

The team's first win in Division One eventually came on 26 November 1983, with new loan signing Danny Crainie, part of Graham's 'wheeling and dealing', delivering two magnificent goals that went towards a 3-1 away win at local rivals West Brom. The win ended a run of 19 games without one and brought Wolves to three points off their next opponents, second from bottom Watford. A win against Graham Taylor's Watford would at least bring them level on points, however it was not to be, with Wolves getting hammered 5-0. By Christmas, the press were regularly speculating about not if, but when, Graham would get the sack. Jane remembers: 'Christmas 1983 was tough but we always had fun - our group of friends at the pub were great and didn't dwell on football. Music and the Woore variety show were talked about the most. I can't remember being very concerned - I had total faith in Graham and that something would turn up.'

The end of December saw the Wolves get two more wins, against Howard Kendall's Everton and Ken Brown's Norwich, and whilst still bottom, the gap was reduced to two points. There was still a glimmer of hope and Graham clung to it. Come January 1984, The FA Cup beckoned, but after two draws against fellow Division One team Coventry, Wolves finally succumbed, losing 3-0 in the third match. January did bring some joy, leading to Richard's favourite quote of his Dad's, when the team beat Liverpool 1-0 at Anfield: 'It feels like winning the cup final, if that's what that feels like!' It was the first time Wolves had done this in 30 years, and it would be another 27 years before the feat were repeated. Graham later told Clive Corbett: 'I went to a good friend's 40th party that evening and they were all Wolves supporters. As I got in, they were all on their knees or bowing and we'd just won one game.' John Griffiths was turning 40, a friend Graham and Jane had met through their dear friend Ray. Jane remembers the party well: 'We were last to arrive due to the game and Graham had a great welcome. Our friends from Wolverhampton who were all Wolves fans were there. It was a great night - we were making the most of the good times again.'

Beating Liverpool, the team that went on to win the league, as well as a brilliant achievement, brought some relief, but the Wolves team wasn't strong enough to perform week in week out at that same level and the pressure started to take its toll on Graham. Rather than sit in the dug-out, he sometimes liked to sit higher up in the stand to get a better view of the game, a practice learned from Graham Turner at Shrewsbury. This meant being in and amongst the fans, who clearly rattled Graham during a game against David Pleat's Luton Town at the end of January. Luton scored the winner four minutes from time, cheered on by the Wolves fans much to Graham's disgust: 'They get on my nerves. They went very quiet when we equalised but the only way I can get back at them is for the team to win. I wonder what they do for fun. That's what worries me. If they've got wives and girlfriends, I wonder what they're like with them? But the women are probably bosses in their homes, they usually are with men like that.' It was an uncharacteristic outburst, but the blatant disloyalty of that handful of fans in the face of such adversity must have hurt: 'who needs enemies with friends like that' springs to mind.

Like David Instone, Barron remembers that the fans' wrath that season in Division One was mostly directed at the Bhatti brothers and/or Dougan, rather than at him and Graham. Perhaps unfairly, there was little anger directed towards Wolverhampton Council who declined planning permission for the supermarket, after local retailers The Mander Centre objected. If the fans on the terraces in 1984 had known that planning permission would ultimately be granted to local developers, Gallagher Estates, to build an Asda supermarket in 1986, in the exact same location that Allied Properties had earmarked, they might have seen it differently, or maybe the Bhattis and Dougan were more suitable pantomime villains than the anonymous figures in brown and grey suits at the council.

The end finally came on 27 April, four days after losing 2-0 away at Everton and sealing their relegation fate. Harrison was with Graham in his office the day the phone call came and remembers he was distraught: 'I don't know if Jane knows this, but I was a smoker at the time and Graham asked me for a cigarette.' Graham had given his all, but it wasn't enough and as is still the way with football managers, had to take the bullet for the team, although, in this case, it was more like he was taking the bullet for the club's owners, the fans, the council who'd refused planning permission as well. Saddled with two mortgages and supporting a young family, Graham was devastated. He later told Clive Corbett: 'To be honest, relegation and my experience at Wolves probably drove me away from management. The crowd didn't know what was going on and I kept my side of the bargain although the directors hadn't said we'd got no money. If they had made that public the club would have folded with creditors flying in. I was getting all kinds of stick, my two boys were little boys and my wife and other family members were there and it was hurtful because the crowd didn't know the true story. My wife and family were magnificent but fortunately we didn't live in the town. Kenny's[22] kids got terrible treatment at school and I know others got the same.'

Graham never spoke badly of Dougan, although he was disappointed that Dougan wasn't the the one to make the call on that fateful day. They remained friends and had met for dinner the week before Dougan's sudden death in 2008. Jane's main complaint goes back to 1967, the year that 'Derek spoiled Christmas'. Dougan's then wife, Jutta, was German and so their family's main celebrations, including sharing presents, took place on Christmas Eve. Dougan asked Jane how she liked her new coat, which of course lay wrapped up intended as a surprise for the following day. 'I never forgave him for spoiling my surprise,' Jane says, with a glint in her eye, and whilst Graham was perhaps more forgiving than our Jane, he'd have preferred to avoid Dougan's surprise that was Tony Towner.

Graham briefly considered selling his story to the press; the money situation was desperate. Harrison was happy to help out, putting out feelers with his contacts in the tabloids, but Graham couldn't do it - he couldn't be disloyal to his club. With two mortgages and the only income coming in from Jane's job at the school, Graham had to sign on at the dole office and experience first-hand the fate suffered by over three million Britons in the early eighties. The contrast could not be more stark. Just one month before he was sacked, Graham had reflected on the rapid fall from grace: 'I am the same manager as last season when everyone was congratulating us on winning promotion. And these are the same players, essentially. A few months ago we were heroes and now we are supposed to be villains.' Harrison remembers his friend Graham as easy-going, happy and positive but the stresses of the 1984 season took their toll. In their lifetime together, Jane recalls only two occasions when Graham lost his temper, both of which occurred during his time as manager at Wolves. The first was at a function in Birmingham, when a journalist suggested that Graham had only been appointed by Dougan as a 'Yes-Man'. The injustice of the comment infuriated Graham and he would have punched said journalist had Doug Hope not intervened. The second was in the Newcastle-Under-Lyme Labour Exchange, when a jobsworth told him he couldn't attend an interview for a football job in Bahrain as he was supposed to be signing on.

With no money to pay him off, Wolves dug their heels in and refused to pay compensation, offering only half of the remainder of Graham's contract. For the second time Graham had to consult a lawyer, and whilst he eventually won the day in court, it would take seven years for Graham to get the money largely because of Wolves' ongoing financial woes. Nevertheless his lawyer, Michael Morrison, became a friend as a result, and being a Manchester-based avid Manchester United fan, would invite Graham to matches in the Executive Suite at Old Trafford in the name of corporate entertaining - even young Richard remembers an invite to one game. Lawyer Morrison proudly related to me that Graham had once described him as: 'the most abusive and noisy football fan he'd ever gone to a match with'. A friendship forged out of adversity, borne of a shared love of the beautiful game.

The end of Graham's time at Wolves, whilst desperately sad, was nonetheless a relief. Graham had been in a hopeless situation. Barron summed up those two seasons for me quite simply: 'It was a great time and a sad time.' Wolves went on to suffer relegation the following three seasons, sliding to the ignominy of the Fourth Division. I asked Harrison if Graham would have succeeded in Division One, had he been backed, and his answer was unequivocal: 'Without a doubt.' Barron echoes Harrison's sentiment, 'Not in a million years should Graham have got the sack.' Barron is also not the only one to feel irked that the league-winning team of 1983 has not been properly honoured, 'One thing that always annoyed me,' he told me, 'was that as far as I know there was never a picture at Molineux of that team that won promotion.' I can only speculate as to why that is - this was the Derek Dougan era and Marmite-figure that he was, subsequent owners of Wolves, including rival bidder Sir Jack Hayward, might have been happy to let the Dougan / Bhatti period be associated with the demise of Wolves that followed, rather than remember the incredible achievement of the team with Graham at the helm. Whilst not acknowledged at Molineux, Graham's family all remain incredibly proud of his achievements at Wolves - brother Andrew explains: 'One of the things that topped it all off was years later, Gail bought me a DVD for my birthday - it was called the history of Wolverhampton Wanderers. In the DVD they interviewed and asked questions to old managers and players. Graham wasn't in the DVD but they asked Andy Gray a question: "Who is the best manager you have ever played under?" His answer was "Graham Hawkins, one of the best and most underestimated managers I have ever worked with, if he had been given the opportunity he would have gone very far". To hear that come out of the mouth of a player of his calibre was amazing. I rang Graham and told him and all he said was "that's nice of him" lol.'

Despite the heartache of 1984, Jane is of the firm view that the best years of their lives as a young family came about as a result of an opportunity borne out of the experience at Wolves. 'Without the Wolves job, we would never have gone to Bahrain.'

A MARRIAGE MADE IN FOOTBALL

Father and son playing together in Bahrain. Back Row L to R:, Ibrahim (Bahraini ex-player), Steve Elliott, Paul Doherty, Daniel Hatfield (later went to Loughborough University like Richard), John Gray, John Gemmill. Front row L to R: Graham, former England captain Kevin Keegan, Kim Barwell, Richard, Hattem Soussi (Tunisian coach).

8 From Woore to War and Back Again

1984 – 1990

In the summer of 1984, Iraq had been at war with Iran for nearly four years, a conflict that would last another four. The Shah of Iran, a Western-friendly leader, had been deposed in 1979 following the Islamic Revolution and replaced with the anti-Western Ayatollah Khomeini and an Islamic Republic. Saddam Hussein, the despotic Iraqi leader, saw an opportunity to invade its neighbour, weakened by the revolution. Britain and the rest of the world looked on nervously, worried about the safety of oil supplies from the Middle East as well as the threat of a rise in Islamic fundamentalism. Bahrain, the Hawkins' family home for six years, sits in the Persian Gulf, a few miles off the coast of oil-rich giant, Saudi Arabia, in waters busy with oil tankers shipping their cargo to the rest of the world. In the eighties, those oil tankers frequently got caught up in the cross-fire of the Iran-Iraq war, and Bahrain was a safe haven for both American and British forces, in situ to try and keep the oil flowing. In July 1984 a BP oil tanker was hit by Iranian missiles just 40 miles north of Bahrain, in May 1987 the Iraqis hit a US frigate killing 28 sailors reputedly by accident and in July 1988, a US navy missile hit an Iranian passenger jet, another accident, killing all 290 civilians on board. However, although Bahrain was located in the middle of a war zone in the eighties, it was not directly involved and life was relatively peaceful for its inhabitants. Indeed, for the six years the family was away, the UK was statistically a much more dangerous place to live, with the IRA subjecting the British mainland to a sustained bombing campaign, almost killing Prime Minister Thatcher and her government at the Brighton Hotel bombing in October 1984.

A MARRIAGE MADE IN FOOTBALL

'When Graham was offered a job in Bahrain, I had to look it up on a map,' Jane confessed and she wouldn't have been the only Brit unfamiliar with this corner of the former British Empire. Back in the eighties, foreign holidays were expensive and places like Bahrain and Dubai were off-the-beaten-track tourist destinations only for the very wealthy. Bahrain certainly wasn't known for its footballing prowess. A small island nation, ruled by the Sunni Muslim Al Khalifa family for over 200 years, Bahrain gained its full independence from Britain in 1971. The Shah of Iran had made a claim to the territory, but the UN stepped in and organised a referendum which gave the mainly Shia-Muslim population two choices: independence or become part of Iran. The Bahrainis voted overwhelmingly for independence.

Post-independence, Bahrain maintained strong links with its former overlord, indeed a British man, Ian Henderson, was head of Bahraini State Security from 1966 to 1998 (with a somewhat dubious record according to Amnesty International, but that's another story). An oil boom in the seventies significantly enriched the nation as its pearl fisheries declined, and its strong ties with Britain resulted in a large ex-pat community on the island, many working in finance, oil as well as infrastructure such as telecoms and engineering. Unlike most other Muslim countries in the Middle East, Bahrain permits the sale and consumption of alcohol and is relatively liberal. Home to Gulf News and Gulf Air, Bahrain was the destination of the first Concorde flight in 1976, a stop-off point for British travellers on the way to the Far East. Whilst for the Hawkins family, life in Bahrain would be very different from what they'd experienced in England, in many respects it felt like an extended holiday.

Graham's job in Bahrain came through a man called Alf D'Arcy. D'Arcy had played non-league football, well-respected by his clubs Barnet FC and Enfield FC, but made a living from organising football tours. From 1901 to 1974 England fielded a national amateur team, and D'Arcy told me that he could have turned professional but that there wasn't enough money in it: 'Bill Nicholson[23] at Spurs approached me but I was a big fish in a small pond and happy with life at Barnet. I doubt very much I would have represented my country so many times or indeed had the opportunity to visit some of the fantastic countries I did had I taken the plunge and gone full time. Anyway the pro wages in those days were nothing like the scale of today's player earnings and I was making a comfortable living with my business interests.' He played over 300 times for Barnet, won over 40 Amateur International Caps, captained his club and country, and travelled all round the world playing football, representing his country at Wembley. D'Arcy told me he'd first met Graham on training courses run by the FA, but they'd first worked together during Graham's time as Wolves manager, as D'Arcy organised their pre-season tours. He got in touch with Graham when an opening came up at a club called Al-Bahrain Sports Club, 'Bahrain SC'. Still in touch with Jane, D'Arcy told me that he didn't hesitate in putting Graham forward for jobs, having placed many high profile former footballers in overseas jobs. 'He was definitely one of the best,' he told me, 'He always had time for people and just got on with the job. Didn't moan and groan like some of them. Always good at his job. Got on with people. Had outstanding relationships with people.'

In 1984, the Bahraini Premier League consisted of just nine clubs with semi-professional players, all of whom had day jobs. Another club, Muharraq, had won the league the previous two years and at the time were the team to beat. English managers were the flavour of the month in Bahrain: Keith Burkinshaw, who had won the UEFA Cup for a second time with Tottenham Hotspur at his final game in charge in 1984, took up his post as manager of the Bahraini National team the following August. Burkinshaw, together with his assistant, Robbie Stepney and physiotherapist, George McAllister, were all familiar, friendly faces for Graham when he first travelled out to take up his new job.

In July 1984, the Hawkinses held the first of their infamous 'open house' events at the bungalow Springbank, an all-day party for over 150 friends and family who dropped in as and when suited. It was a chance to say goodbye before embarking on their Middle Eastern adventure. Graham set off alone initially, and the plan was that Jane would travel over with the boys in September. A few weeks in and Graham was finding the adjustment difficult without his wife and family, 'Graham said that if we didn't join him soon he would come home,' Jane recalls, so their departure was brought forward a little.

However, almost as soon as Jane and the boys touched down in their new homeland, Graham flew off on a pre-season tour to the country then known as the Yemen Arab Republic ('YAR' or North Yemen). North Yemen was separated from its southern neighbour, the People's Republic of Democratic Yemen between 1962 and 1990, when they unified as The Republic of Yemen. North Yemen, a country beset with civil war for decades, had a football team that hadn't competed since 1966, but were seeking to reinvigorate its fortunes in 1984 and launched a bid to qualify for the 1984 Asian Cup. Graham's pre-season trip with Bahrain SC to the capital of North Yemen, San'aa, probably came with financial incentives. Jane recalls Graham's tales of his trip to the walled city, where women didn't venture out on the streets, where every adult male carried a traditional, ornamental dagger known as a janbiyya, its handle made of rhino horn, an important status symbol. Yemen was then and is now an incredibly poor country, ravaged by war over many generations. Princess Anne visited in early 1984 as patron of the Save the Children charity - although this was not a place many westerners ever set foot. On this trip and throughout his time at Bahrain SC, Graham was eternally grateful to his assistant, Youssef Hamdan who provided invaluable advice on Arab ways and culture as well as translation. Jane remembers Hamdan giving them a copy of the Koran in English and became a good friend during their time in Bahrain. On one occasion, Hamdan invited the Hawkins family to his home, where they met his wife and two young children. The men entertained in one room, with the women partaking of their fruit juice and 7Up in another. Jane duly sat cross-legged on the floor together with the women, understanding none of the chatter, but appreciative of the women's beautifully-coloured dresses, normally covered by the black abaya when outside of the home.

By the end of August, the Hawkins family of four was installed in the first of four different homes in Bahrain, a villa with a shared pool on a compound in Budaiya, in the northwest of the island, just to the west of the capital, Manama. Graham was paid enough for the family to live comfortably, school fees for the boys at an international school were also funded as was one return flight back a year to the UK for the family, but this was no millionaire's lifestyle. Flights back to the UK were expensive and there wasn't enough money around to travel back very easily. Jane remembers the ex-pat bankers in Bahrain as a set distinct from their own circle; they had their own club ('The Bankers' Club') and enjoyed greater trappings of wealth than the footballing community, often employing a number of servants.

Jane describes a typical day in their life in the sun back then: 'Graham and I would take boys to school then go into Manama and meet other coaches for coffee, or go home and sit by the pool, Graham would prepare the coaching session for the evening. Graham played tennis and squash with others and also go to the National Stadium with George[24] to help with injuries. We were members of the Dilmun Club[25] so spent some time there swimming and eating. Afternoons we would collect the boys from school and take Graham to Muharraq for training. If there was not enough time to go home, then Graham would drive himself to training and the boys would go to the pool after doing their homework. Weekends were full of sport and socialising, and trips to the Sheikh's beach.'

The Sheikh's beach was on the East coast and at that time, was the only beach on the island. Ex-pats were invited to partake freely of the facilities there (so long as their skin was white), but required to hand over any cameras to the armed guards who hung them on the palm trees for collection on exit. Pretty young girls were invited to take tea with the emir, Sheikh Isa, and he would stroll up and down the beach in his thobe (long, white smock) before making his selection. For the Hawkins family, the Sheikh's beach was a fun weekend outing, the boys thrilled with fizzy drinks on tap, playing in the sea on the surfboards. As a married lady with children, Jane was never invited to tea with the Sheikh - he was more interested in the Gulf Air hostesses. One rumour abounding was that the number of gold bracelets adorning the girls' wrists was indicative of their number of invites to tea.

Bahrain was a sociable time - Jane and Graham made many great friends through ex-pat clubs. Initially, this was the Dilmun Club

A MARRIAGE MADE IN FOOTBALL

and later on, at the British 'Brit' Club, where Graham became 'Sports Member', meaning he was responsible for organising a variety of sporting events, including regular 'England v Scotland' football matches. Some of the naval ships docking in Bahrain also had cocktail parties and in true colonial style, Jane and Graham got to dress up and hobnob with the military. Later on in their stay, Graham and the Brit Club played in a football match against the crew of the HMS Diligence, a British warship that would go on to carry out mine-sweeping operations at the end of the Iran-Iraq war in 1988 as well as serve in the Gulf War of 1990.

Once the boys were settled into their new school, Jane took up a job in a nursery school, looking after a small group of toddlers every morning. Whilst she enjoyed spending time with the children, relations between the staff and the owner of the school weren't good, so after a couple of months she left and took up an administrative post at Dilmun School, where she stayed for the rest of their time in Bahrain. Football life was good too - and Graham's first season in charge of Bahrain SC went well. Graham overcame both language and cultural barriers with the help of his trusty assistant, Hamdan, and Bahrain SC went on to win the league, overcoming the previous champions Muharraq in dramatic fashion. In a league-deciding fixture in February 1985, Bahrain SC took the lead against Muharraq, but after some dubious refereeing the challengers were denied a penalty and in the six minutes of unwarranted extra time Muharraq equalised. Tempers rose and the Muharraq goalkeeper threw a punch at Graham's jaw. After a trip to the police station the following day to give a statement, the game was replayed and Bahrain SC came out on top, sealing the league title with a victory over Al Hala a couple of weeks later.

Celebrations for the league success abounded, Bahraini-style. The first event was at Bahrain SC club house, where again Jane found that she was the only female present. She remembers one of the players bringing a flat drum, many of them dancing in a circle to its rhythm, at one point dragging Ian up, who, unlike his more bashful brother, was more than happy to join in. Some of the men balanced Bahraini coffee pots on their heads as they danced. They celebrated more formally at a popular restaurant, Sizzlers, but on this occasion

Graham invited their friends from the British Club, Maree and husband Glyn McCarthy (always referred to as 'Macca'), so at least Jane had some female company.

After winning the league, Graham's job at Bahrain SC was secure for the next season and with the boys settled in school, life was good. However, the distance from family and friends back in the UK could be incredibly painful at times. One day Graham received a devastating phone call in Bahrain letting him know that his friend from Lytham, Dave, husband to Chris and father to Stephen, Gavin and Andrew, had taken his own life. Richard remembers his Dad being upset, 'Dad was never upset,' and later his Mum explaining why. The prohibitive cost of flights back to the UK meant that travelling back for the funeral was not possible, and the family had to mourn the loss of their friend thousands of miles away. Jane and Chris remain close friends to this day, as do Richard and the boys - all big football fans - connecting each year through their Fantasy Football league. That same year, in May 1985, another devastating phone call came, this time from Jane's brother David to tell her that their mother had had a stroke. The boys were still at school and so when Graham accompanied Jane on the flight back to the UK, fellow Brit manager of Bahraini club Al-Qadisiya, Brian Doyle, moved into the villa to take care of them. Doyle had been in the Middle East for some time - Dave Mackay[26], who went out to manage Kuwaiti club Al-Arabi in 1978 and stayed there for eight years, talks about meeting and befriending Doyle in his book written together with Martin Knight, 'The Real Mackay'. Jane attests to Doyle being a lovely man, and Richard remembers Doyle and Burkinshaw's assistant Robbie Stepney as a bit of a double act, always telling jokes and making everyone laugh.

Graham returned to Bahrain alone to finish the season and take care of the boys. Sadly they wouldn't see their grandmother again as she died on 9th June 1985, before they got back to the UK. It must have been a difficult time for Jane to be away from her beloved husband and children. Richard remembers his maternal grandmother fondly: 'She always had her pinny on, was always cooking. I remember she had those big Dame Edna glasses.' During the Bahrain years, the long summer holidays were spent in the bungalow at Woore and the family escaped the excessive heat of Bahrain during those months. It was a chance to see family and friends, and that summer after her mother's death, Jane appreciated being able to spend an extended period with Dad, Samuel.

The family returned together to Bahrain in September 1985, and after an initial hiccup when the boys school fees hadn't been paid by Bahrain SC, they settled back into the rhythms of life in the sun. Long hot days ended with the call to prayer from the mosque, which for both Jane and Richard, evokes magical memories of their time in Bahrain. Other local customs remained incomprehensible, and none more so than the practice of flagellation practised by some Shia Muslims during the festival of Ashura in October. The majority (approximately 90%) of the world's Muslim population are Sunni Muslims, but around 10% are Shia and form the majority of the muslim populations of Bahrain, Iran and Azerbaijan. The Shia believe that Ali (Shia comes from 'Shiat Ali' - 'The Party of Ali') was the rightful successor to the Prophet Mohammed upon his death in the seventh century. Ali and his son Hassan were killed in separate assassinations in 661CE and 680CE respectively, whilst Ali's second son Hussein was killed in a bloody battle in 681CE alongside many of his fellow Shia Muslims. It is Hussein's death that gives rise to the Shia concept of martyrdom - for Sunni Muslims Ashura is a more joyful affair, celebrating Moses freeing the Israelites from the Pharaoh by parting the Red Sea, marked by fasting rather than blood-letting. The sight of men's bloodied shirts from whipping, often with chains adorned with blades, shocked Jane as they drove the boys home through Jidhafs, a relatively poor district in Bahrain. Many Shia Muslim clerics have sought to discourage the gory custom, encouraging blood donation as a more community-minded commemoration.

In October 1985, Graham went on a short trip to Baghdad together with his club, league champions Bahrain SC and the runners-up, Muharraq. Keith Burkinshaw, manager of the Bahraini national team came too. All too aware of the close links between politics and football, Jane was relieved to hear that the Bahraini teams lost to their Iraqi counterparts, knowing things might have got a bit 'sticky' if the Iraqi teams had lost. Dave Mackay, whilst manager of Al-Arabi in

Kuwait, tells the story of the murder of Sheikh Fahad, one of the patrons of Al-Arabi, the half-brother of the Emir of Kuwait and someone he remembers fondly. In 1990, when Saddam Hussein's Iraqi army invaded Kuwait, his equally brutal son, Uday, reportedly personally shot Sheikh Fahd. Sheikh Fahd's Kuwaiti national team had previously beaten Iraq in a so-called friendly match and Uday took his revenge with a bullet. On that trip to Baghdad, Graham shared a taxi with Uday Hussein - he would not have known at that time the full extent of the evil this man was capable of - revealed to the world many years later, when Saddam Hussein and his cronies were deposed in 2003. With Saddam imprisoned awaiting trial, Uday fled and Iraqi footballers finally felt safe enough to speak out about the atrocities they'd suffered at the hands of the regime. There are tales horrific torture, carefully concealed from visiting FIFA officials, personally dealt out by Uday Hussain, chairman of the Iraqi football federation. Players were imprisoned for missing training sessions, regardless of the reason and anything other than a win meant beatings for the players. 'Motivational' speeches from Uday comprised threats of violence and mutilation.

Burkinshaw returned from Baghdad to find his wife traumatised by a burglar - Jane recalls: 'Joyce, his wife, fought off an attack - she screamed so much he left and she lost her voice for days. Never knew who it was but they knew Keith was away with the team.' Nonetheless, burglary and other such crimes were rare in Bahrain and didn't blight the Hawkins family - Jane recalls the sole guard who sat outside their complex in Budaiya. A few months later, in March 1986, the Arabian Gulf Cup was held in Bahrain, but unfortunately for the Burkinshaws, the host nation finished only fifth out of seven nations; Burkinshaw's contract wasn't renewed and the family returned to football life in the UK. That same month, Ian and Richard got their own opportunity to play international football when their school took them on tour to play football at a tournament in Doha, capital of nearby Qatar and a short flight away. Like Bahrain, Qatar was formerly a British Protectorate, achieved independence in 1971 and has been ruled by the same family (the House of Thani) for over two hundred years. Ranked third in the world in terms of wealth per capita (behind Saudi Arabia and the UAE) due to its oil reserves, Qatar punches above its weight internationally, is known for its TV network, Al Jazeera, as well as being the first Middle Eastern venue for the Football World Cup, due to be held in 2022.

The following month, Graham was off with Bahrain SC on a two week trip to Riyadh, Saudi Arabia for the Gulf Champions Cup, the Middle Eastern equivalent of the European Champions League. Saudi Arabia dwarfs Bahrain in size of both land mass and economy, and the trip was certainly an eye-opener for Graham together with physio George McAllister, who also came to support the team. A Saudi club, Al-Hilal, went on to win the tournament, but it was the corporate entertainment on offer that was more memorable than the football. After one match, Graham and his team were invited to witness a beheading, an invitation he politely declined, unlike his team and all of the officials.

Back home, Bahrain SC was not able to repeat their league win, with their rivals Muharraq taking the 1986 title. With Ian finishing school that summer and moving to a boarding school in England to take 'A' Levels which were not offered by his International School in Bahrain, Graham's employers wanted the family to find cheaper accommodation for the three of them and the family rented a flat in the centre of town, just across the road from the British Club. This was to be Jane's favourite home in Bahrain, with friends Maree and Macca upstairs, Jan and Tony downstairs, there was much socialising between the three homes. After another 'open house' party at Springbank, catching up with UK family and friends, Graham travelled out to Bahrain alone, with Jane following three weeks later together with Richard after tearful farewells to Ian as he started sixth form as a boarder at school in Oswestry. In November, Cornwall friends Joe Mercer and Gwen came to stay for a three week holiday, distracting Jane from her missing elder son and as they flew out, Prince Charles and Princess Diana visited the island, taking in the newly opened King Fahd Causeway. The 25km bridge connected the island of Bahrain to Saudi Arabia. Jane remembers the opening: 'My friend's husband was in the police and told us that the Bahraini jails were full of drunken Saudis on the weekends. They would come across with crates of empty bottles, fill them up with alcohol and return home.' Saudi Arabia, unlike Bahrain, was (and still is) a dry country, with severe penalties for anyone found consuming alcohol.

The 1987 league title went to West Riffa and Bahrain SC informed Graham that his services would not be required for the following season. The family were not yet ready to leave their island paradise and Graham duly attended an interview at Al-Hala club. A new job secured, they then had to secure accommodation and the family's third home in Bahrain was a small villa in Al A'Ali, near the national stadium, somewhat less salubrious than earlier accommodation and some way from local amenities. Still, the weather remained wonderful, and Bahrain was a small island with everything reachable in a short drive.

When the family were reunited in the UK that summer, Richard got his first shot at a footballing career, having impressed former Tottenham Hotspur coach, Robbie Stepney. Stepney had been Burkinshaw's assistant at Spurs and still had strong links with the club. Stepney organised for Richard to spend a few weeks in the summer holidays training with the Spurs youth team as a 14 year old, where he remembers seeing the talent in 13 year old Jamie Redknapp as well as meeting manager Terry Venables. The following summer, in July 1988, Richard spent a couple of weeks training at Mick Mills' Stoke City, at that time a Division Two club where Graham had many contacts. Richard was relatively tall for his age, and used to playing football with fully-grown men at the British Club with his older brother and Dad, and a promising footballer. He'd also been a regular at training in Bahrain with his Dad, delivering crosses into the box to help the team practice set pieces. After playing with some of the footballing stars of the future in England, back in Bahrain in April 1988, Richard got the opportunity to play with some of the footballing stars of the past. George Best, Kevin Keegan, Pat Jennings and Dutch legend Johnny Rep all came out to Bahrain to play in a testimonial event. Richard remembers Kevin Keegan giving him his boots, George Best sadly being too drunk to play and Pat Jennings having his bible stolen from the Juffair Dome where the games were played. I asked Richard what happened to footballing legend, Kevin Keegan's boots and ever pragmatic, he replied: 'I gave them away. They were size six and too small.'

Securing a second season at Al-Hala was uncertain and Graham hadn't enjoyed coaching there as much as at Bahrain SC and so he started to look around for his next move. In April 1988, he travelled to Kuwait for an interview for a job with Al-Fahaheel FC in Kuwait City which was not successful but gave him at least an opportunity to take a look around. Ultimately Al-Hala renewed his contract for another year, but it would be the last. Back in the UK for the summer, Graham toyed with the idea of buying a sports centre in nearby Stone, before pulling out, realising it would cost too much.

1988 was Richard's last year in Bahrain and in September, he followed his older brother to the sixth form at Oswestry School, leaving Jane and Graham to return to their jobs in Bahrain without either of the boys for the first time, reunited again only at Christmas. January 1989 saw Ian start his first job as a financial advisor in Wolverhampton. Graham was in the UK with Ian as his Dad, Ernie, having struggled with his health for several months, sadly passed away. As Jane was working in Bahrain, Graham was without his beloved wife when he lost his father and returning to Bahrain at the end of January, there was more bad news waiting for him. The job at Al-Hala had not been as successful as his time at Bahrain Club and mid-February, issues came to a head when only one of the team turned up to training. At a meeting with the Club's President, Graham was asked to step down and act as an advisor to the Bahraini coach Saad, an offer which was angrily rejected. Meanwhile, Jane's father Samuel, who had been living in a residential home for just over a year, took a turn for the worse and Jane flew to the UK to see him. Just under two weeks later, Samuel passed away as Jane was on the plane back to Bahrain. Unable to afford another flight back to attend the funeral, Jane didn't go, causing some family upset at the time. Ian and Richard, both in the UK, went together, mourning the last of their surviving grandparents.

With no likelihood of Al-Hala renewing Graham's contract, if the couple were to stay in Bahrain, Graham needed to find a new job. Jane's salary at Dilmun School wasn't enough to support them both and pay Richard's school fees, and they relied on Graham's employer to fund their accommodation. At the end of April 1988 he attended an interview for a games teacher role at Ibn Khaldoon school and faced a month-long wait before learning that he was successful. After a holiday with friends at their relatives' home on the Bosphorus in Turkey, their first since arriving in Bahrain, Jane and Graham returned to the UK in July of 1989, before returning to Bahrain in September. After a term as a school-teacher, Graham realised this was not what he had come to Bahrain to do and on 22nd December, after six years abroad, they packed up their belongings and returned to the UK.

Alf D'Arcy, who'd set up Graham for his first job in Bahrain, had some work for him upon his return to the UK. Initially this was accompanying different national teams on tour in Europe, in playing friendly matches as part of their preparations for the 1990 World Cup that was to be held in Italy. January 1990 took Graham to France and Saudi Arabia, leaving Jane on her own back in the UK. When a job came up in February accompanying the Polish national team to Egypt for a match against Kuwait (funded by Kuwait), Graham asked if Jane could come along and so Jane got to see first-hand what Graham was up to as well as do a little sightseeing. Unfortunately she succumbed to food poisoning, as seems to be a pre-requisite of any trip to Egypt. The teams played at the Zamelek stadium in Cairo (drawing 1-1) before heading north on a coach up to Alexandria for the second planned game. After torrential rain, the pitch in Alexandria was sodden and unplayable, but as the Polish team wouldn't be paid if they didn't play and after a few frantic phone calls, the Kuwaitis agreed to pay for the teams to train instead.

On her return to the UK, Jane had found work in the coffee shop at Bridgemere Garden Centre nearby, although a financially life-changing job offer for Graham meant that she handed in her notice a few months later. Again through Alf D'Arcy, Graham had been offered a lucrative contract to manage the Kuwaiti Club, Al-Arabi, the club previously managed by Dave Mackay for six years. Mackay talks about his salary negotiation with Al-Arabi in his book when he was offered the job in 1978, which basically involved them giving him what he asked for, which gross was about three times what he could have earned in the UK, but significantly more than that in net terms, given it was tax-free. Mackay had also asked for a £12,000 up front cash payment which was duly paid without a quibble.

Having lived in the Middle East for over six years, Jane knew full well where Kuwait was and had friends who had lived there. She felt excited about the move: 'The money was the pull and a couple of years would have been great. Yes it was dry, but the expats managed to cope somehow. I wasn't worried about anything - it was another adventure.' Back in 1982, England World Cup winner, Geoff Hurst, had gone out to Kuwait to manage the second biggest side, Kuwait Sporting City, and in an interview with Sport360, told of his experiences which sound similar to those of Graham in Bahrain. Hurst tells of the challenges of instilling professionalism in the players and ensuring disciplinary measures were enforceable, in a world where players all had day-jobs. Once authority was established, with no contractual issues with players or scouting responsibilities, it was just about the football - training and setting up for matches.

Graham's first task as Al-Arabi coach was pre-season training in Wiesbaden, west of Frankfurt and it would be another holiday for Jane as the Kuwaitis were happy for her to tag along. Whilst Jane was checking out the shops, Saddam Hussein had other plans. The Iran-Iraq war had now ended in a stalemate and Iraq had nothing to show for its efforts other than a significant loss of life and mounting financial debts. Those debts included a $14 billion loan from Iraq's neighbour Kuwait, who had supported Iraq as indeed had the West, in an attempt to halt a rise in Islamic Fundamentalism in the Middle East fuelled by Iran. The war over, Kuwait's support did not extend to forgiving the debt and this disagreement, combined with Saddam Hussein's empire-building desires and arguments over oil production, led to the Iraqi tanks pouring into Kuwait in August 1990. Graham was with the Al-Arabi squad when the devastating news came through and the young men were all immediately desperately concerned about the safety of their families back home. Every day brought a new story of atrocities committed by Iraqi soldiers and dashes for the border as the many ex-pats living in Kuwait tried to escape. A British Airways plane, stopping in Kuwait to re-fuel en route to Singapore, got stuck in the war zone and as the weeks dragged on, relatives became anxious as the papers were rife with rumours of western hostages to be used as human shields by the Iraqis at military targets. Graham would never get his lucrative contract and he wasn't the only one - Mick Mills[27], having being sacked by Stoke City (where Richard had trained one summer), had been due to fly out to take up a job at Kuwait Sporting City, said simply: 'I've been very unlucky, but compared with people in Kuwait, it's minor.'

Jane and Graham never did hit the football jackpot, but truly it was a lucky escape. Kuwait was finally liberated in February 1991, after a massive six week assault by US-led coalition forces and a seven month occupation. For many of those trapped in Kuwait, the mental scars of their experience would never heal.

A MARRIAGE MADE IN FOOTBALL

Charity nights at the Coopers Arms: Wolves legend Eddie Clamp to the left of Graham, England legend Sir Stanley Matthews on the right. Clamp and Matthews played together at Stoke City in the sixties.

9 If You Marry a Footballer...You'll End Up in a Pub

1990 – 1998

Jane and Graham returned home from Wiesbaden and their brief time with Al-Arabi, deeply troubled by the news and concerned for the fates of the young men returning home to Kuwait. Their adventure in the Middle East was over and after six years away, they returned to the UK to see what football in the nineties had to offer. They had been away for two major events that would shape English football, namely the Heysel Stadium disaster in 1985 and the Hillsborough disaster in 1989. Football fans died in crushes at both events, football fans were initially blamed for both events and it would take decades of fighting in the courts for the families of the Hillsborough victims before evidence of a cover-up of the failings of the South Yorkshire police was revealed to the public. UEFA determined that the deaths of mostly Juventus fans in Heysel were caused by Liverpool fans, and banned English clubs from European football. That ban was finally lifted for the 1990/91 season. The Taylor Report, published in January 1990, judged that the Hillsborough disaster was caused by a failure of police control and resulted in the requirement of all major clubs to provide all-seater stadiums, the cost of which required significant investment. The very top clubs in English football would at least be able to access the income stream that the European tournaments offered, but all league clubs were saddled with the financial responsibility of upgrading stadia[28].

A MARRIAGE MADE IN FOOTBALL

Wolverhampton Wanderers had had a turbulent time since Graham's departure in 1984. After dropping to Division Two, they had sunk to Division Four and again fallen into receivership after which, Graham's old boss, Graham Turner took on the managerial job in 1986. This time Wolverhampton Council bought the stadium and duly awarded the contract to a local developer to build a supermarket on the adjoining land. Unsurprisingly, with the council on the hook for making Wolves a going concern, they awarded planning permission this time. Graham Turner, together with the goals of Steve Bull, guided them back up the ladder, at least up to Division Two by 1990. Sir Jack Hayward then bought them in May 1990 and would provide the funding they needed to update the stadium to meet the requirements of the Taylor Report. The combination of Sir Jack Hayward and Graham Turner at Wolves must have seemed like a bizarre alternative reality for our Graham - he came back to the UK to find that his childhood club was managed by the Graham the press had thought was the new boss back in 1982 and owned by the bidder who had been favourite to win the bidding war then, as if the Bhatti brothers had never happened.

Graham's second club, Preston North End, like many clubs outside of the top tier, had had a tough time in the eighties. Gordon Lee, Graham's former boss at Blackburn managed them for a while, as did Irish goalkeeper and Graham's Preston team-mate Alan Kelly, but having started the decade out in the third tier, they were propping up the bottom of the Fourth Division by 1986, and applying for re-election to the football league. By 1990, Preston had made it back up to Division Three, but wouldn't progress any higher until 2000. Blackburn, Graham's other club in the North West, like Preston was competing for revenue with some of the country's biggest clubs, and regularly saw attendances slump to less than 5,000 during the eighties. Blackburn had started out the eighties in the second tier and came close to promotion at times, but never quite made it. Nonetheless, Blackburn was in much better shape than Preston, staying relatively safe in Division Two at the time of Graham's return to the UK.

In the period after returning from Bahrain, and before the Al-Arabi opportunity presented itself, Graham was back at Blackburn, tasked with setting up a scouting network. When Graham was manager of Wolves, he and his coaching staff (of two) did most of the scouting themselves, but in the early nineties this was starting to change. Scouting involves watching football, a lot of football, either checking out the opposition in advance of a fixture (tactical scouting) or watching individual players with a view to unearthing young talent. Jane remembers going along to do a spot of shopping when Graham was at matches. She recalls: 'Graham made lots of notes on his match programmes. Looked like hieroglyphics to me.' Richard, in 1990 enrolled on a sports science degree course at Loughborough, remembers going along to matches to scout with his Dad, contributing by watching players in certain set plays. Over the years Graham scouted for a number of clubs, including Wolves. One young player who particularly impressed him was a teenage Michael Carrick, who would go on to play and coach at Manchester United with Richard.

Whilst researching this period in Graham's life, Richard handed me a book from 2014 by sports journalist Michael Calvin, 'The Nowhere Men', which explores the lives of the football scouts. It was a book Graham enjoyed greatly and was the last book he finished just before he died. 'The Nowhere Men' is a wonderful tribute to the hidden underclass of today's football, an army of men working for a pittance for the love of the beautiful game, many of them former players like Graham. Whilst the world of scouting has evolved considerably since 1990 with the increasing role of data analysts combined with the spending power of the Premier League clubs, there is still a role for the 'flat cap brigade' who provide the expertise and insight that data crunching cannot deliver. This expertise is sadly grossly undervalued and loyalty typically unappreciated. Graham didn't have such gripes with Blackburn, a generally well-run club that tried to look after its players and employees, but it was nonetheless a tough business. As well as scouting for Blackburn, Graham along with other former players would travel to Blackburn on match-days for 'entertaining' at his old haunt, the 100 Club. He was required to chat about football to fans and whilst not particularly well-paid, was something he enjoyed and a helpful networking opportunity.

A MARRIAGE MADE IN FOOTBALL

Graham enjoyed being back at Blackburn, but the Al-Arabi offer was too lucrative to turn down. It was a chance to feel financially secure for the rest of their lives. Who knows how things could have panned out differently if Graham had stayed at Blackburn, as just a year later, in January 1991, it was announced that Jack Walker had taken control of the club. Walker, a life-long supporter, was a Jersey-based multi-millionaire who had made his fortune, alongside his brother Fred, in the development of Walker Steel in Blackburn. In October 1991 Walker installed footballing legend Kenny Dalgleish as manager and by 1992, Blackburn were in the top flight of football, now the illustrious Premier League, and paying top dollar for Alan Shearer, still the leading goal-scorer of all time in the Premier League.

After the Al-Arabi job fell through, whilst Jane was able to take back her old job at the garden centre at Bridgemere: 'I did full time, working in the coffee shop and the wholesale plant dept, typing etc. I really loved my time at Bridgemere', Graham's role as Chief Scout at Blackburn had been filled although he did scout local matches for his successor as well as for Wolves. It was around this time, that Graham's younger brother Andrew, started coaching an adult Sunday league team in his home town of Wolverhampton, and with a bit of time on his hands, Graham was happy to help out his little brother. Andrew remembers: 'As I got older, late 20s early 30s, I used to manage and coach an adult Sunday morning league team. All the players were from off the estates Graham had lived in. Some knew him and the rest had heard of him. One Saturday afternoon in June, Graham rang me and asked how we had got on last season and all the normal chat, then he said "When are you starting pre-season training?". I said "Tomorrow morning. Why?". He said "Do you want any help?". I said "In what way?". He said "Do you want me to come over and help you with the training?". My reply was: "WHAT?! Are you serious?". He said "Yes, what time?". I replied "10am, Bentley Leisure Pavilion, the old Rubery Owens[29] to you, don't be late". You should have seen my players' faces when he got out of his car - they were buzzing. They were saying to me: "what's your brother doing here?", I hadn't pre-warned them: "He is here to coach you lot". They couldn't believe it. They absolutely loved the training session, in which he taught me a hell of a lot that day. But that was the type of person he was. That day will never leave me.'

The scouting, the corporate hospitality role at Blackburn and Jane's earnings from the Bridgemere garden centre were not enough to sustain Graham and Jane financially (plus one son in full-time education), and so Graham looked for another job. The opportunity came through his football network, in the form of John Ritchie, a former Stoke (and Sheffield Wednesday) player. Ritchie had enjoyed a successful First Division career as a forward, and with 176 goals for Stoke City, remains their all-time top striker. In 1972 Ritchie started his wholesale business, supplying crockery to hotels, restaurants and care homes; he'd focused on it full-time after a broken leg ended his playing career in 1974. Graham was employed by Ritchie's company as a door-to-door pottery salesman. Richard recalls how during this time his Dad would always turn the plates upside down if they ever went out for a pub meal, checking the brand printed on the underside.

Graham, by nature somewhat shy, was not a natural salesman. Happy to talk for many hours about football and other subjects he was interested in, selling pottery whilst do-able was not enjoyable and he started to consider other options. When Graham and Jane heard that their friends Eric and Olwyn were planning on retiring from the Coopers Arms in Woore, the seeds of an idea were sewn. Using the money Jane had inherited from her parents, in October 1991 Jane and Graham took on the lease of the Coopers Arms. Jane explains: 'When we first applied for a pub we were offered one in Stoke, absolutely no way, but a pub like the Coopers doesn't get offered to first timers. With Eric pushing we managed to get it. So I guess we were lucky, but here started some very hard work and very long hours, After five plus years holiday in the Gulf it was a bit of a shock.' Eric and Olwyn had become good friends of the couple and did what they could to help them take over the pub when they retired. Graham also worked behind the bar to get a feel for the job. Jane smiles wryly when she recalls her mother's words to her as a teenager in love: 'If you marry a footballer, you'll end up in a pub.' It was a well-trodden route by former footballers - former Shrewsbury Town captain, Jake King[30], ran a pub just outside Shrewsbury, The Cross Gates, and they would visit each other occasionally, and swap notes.

The local paper did a spread on the former footballing hero going into the pub trade with the headline: 'Oh What a Lovely Woore' (referencing Kuwait), and quoted Graham: 'It promises to be very hard work but we're very keen to give it a go because it's something we've always talked about over the years. In many ways it's more demanding than soccer management, but we are both relishing the challenge.'

He wasn't wrong about the hard work, it was relentless. Jane recalls: 'We never had a day off for the first 18 months, there was no one to cover for me. My regular outing was the cash'n'carry which I didn't like doing. Then I got in touch with a girl I worked with at Bridgemere, Helen Seabridge, she was a very confident girl and home from uni, which she didn't like so packed it in and worked for us full time. I could trust her to do everything correctly, her boyfriend would come and stay with her and we then managed to stay at the bungalow Sunday nights and have Mondays off. Helen was my saviour. David came to cover for Graham when the coal trade was slow in the summer and Angela and Paul would come for the weekend. Paul was about nine or ten years old then. In 1995 we went to Javea[31] for Macca's 40th and Richard came too. Other times we just had time at the bungalow and go out days to have lunch.' Other than the trip to Javea, Graham and Jane were not able to holiday together. They both returned to Bahrain to visit friends, but separately. Graham took his treasured video camera with him, making films of their old haunts to show Jane on his return.

Like the Egyptians, Jane and Graham's years of feast and leisure in the Middle East preceded their years of famine slogging away in the pub, although that order of events is typical of a footballer's lot. Working in the pub was incessant and not particularly lucrative. Jane remember's Graham would get incredibly frustrated at times, 'He would go into the cellar and just scream.' Everything revolved around the pub and other than Mondays, there was no escape, although they did become very close to their neighbours and customers. Jane recalls:

'I knew everyone in Woore, working at the school and different clubs and activities really helped. Graham knew a few but soon knew everyone. It took me a while to feel confident behind the bar. I knew it was long hours and hard work but with us both working and keeping staff to a minimum, we were able to start saving again. The worst bit was when friends would pop in for a drink on their way to a party, function or even going to eat at another pub.'

Jane and Graham would not be alone for long in the pub, however, as an unexpected addition to the family came one evening to the bungalow. Ben the Saluki, a breed of dog originating from the Middle East known as a 'gift from Allah', turned up on Jane and Graham's doorstep. Jane tells the tale: 'He stayed the night with us and the next day Graham took him a walk down by the quarry across the fields behind the bungalow. He met this guy looking for his dog, he didn't really want him but was worried in case he was hurt.' Word must have got out in the dog world and one bonfire night Hector the Cairn Terrier arrived in the pub. Jane recalls: 'He had bolted from his home in Pipegate, one mile from Woore. Being so close we found his owners and they had a young son and the mum was in the early stages of MS so another conversation and we kept him.' By now, Graham and Jane had a bit of a reputation and when a retired greyhound was spotted wandering in the village, many of the locals called up, thinking she belonged to the Hawkins family. Jane remembers: 'Graham was seeing the accountant in Wolverhampton so I took Ben out on the lead to try and get the greyhound to come to me. So when Graham arrived back she was well in with the staff and bar regulars.' Graham chose the name for dog number three, 'Blossom', a character from one of his favourite films, 'Highlander'. The dogs quickly settled into pub life, although they had very different characters. Hector in particular was fiercely loyal to Graham, and was known to nip various visitors, including Richard and Ian, if he felt his time with his lord and master was threatened.

Jane described how they divided up their duties: 'We opened every day, and were generally up at 7am. I would walk the dogs with a friend and Graham sorted out the beer and dealt with orders and invoices. I would prepare food for lunch. We had lots of regular customers even to the point where we knew what they would be eating, where they would sit. Graham would walk the dogs while I closed up and then we would have couple of hours in the flat upstairs, listen to music and have a nap. Six pm open up, food finished at nine pm then I would go and change and help Graham till closing time. We also did outside bars for private parties and charity evenings. Graham played for the dominoes team, and darts when they were short. I also helped out when the ladies' darts team were short.'

It was hard work, but Graham and Jane still knew how to have fun. Jane recalls: 'During our time in the pub we did have many memorable times, our 25th wedding anniversary, dress as you did in the sixties, our 50th birthdays and many organised music evenings and lots of impromptu ones.' Whilst pub life took up most of Graham's time, he remained in touch with his football networks. Derek Fazackerley, Graham's great friend from Blackburn days, would visit regularly and Derek Dougan would pop in from time to time. Graham was also somewhat of a local celebrity, and unsurprisingly, the pub was a haven for football chat. There were also football-related events Jane remembers: 'At that time there was still a beautiful ballroom at Trentham and Graham went to many boxing do's there, usually men only. It was the place for big events then. Also there were special events at Stoke City - one special one was Sir Stan's[32] 80th Birthday.'

During the pub years, Ian was forging a successful career as a financial advisor, and whilst he did play some non-league football and earned a little money doing so, he was not going to follow in his father's footsteps onto the pitch. Meanwhile at boarding school in Oswestry until 1990, Richard continued to enjoy playing football, with some success as school captain as well as playing for Shropshire. His time playing for his county brought some tough opponents - he remembers Merseyside were always a strong team, and a match against Manchester saw him play against a particularly talented player called Ryan (known as Wilson in the nineties, taking his mother's name of Giggs when he was 16.) Richard was invited to attend an England schoolboy trial aged 17, but didn't quite make it. 'I wanted to play full back, and I might have stood a chance at that position, but I was playing centre forward, where I played for the county. I just wasn't good enough as a centre forward at that level.' After finishing his 'A' Levels in 1990, a sports science degree at Loughborough beckoned and Richard continued to play competitive football for his university. University life suited him, and he stayed on to complete a Masters after finishing his degree and then a PhD after that. 'To be honest, we did wonder if he'd ever leave and get a proper job!' Jane laughs. Football would be Richard's life-long passion, but along a different path to that of his father. After suffering a serious injury to his quad muscle whilst on trial for Leicester City Reserves when still a student, his chance at a professional career was over. Ever modest and philosophical, Richard has no regrets. Jane sees Richard's football injuries in a typically positive light: 'He did pick up injuries fairly easily but the Leicester trial we felt was made worse with them not having the knowledge to deal with the injury. It was early days in the process of sports injuries and some I guess still believed in the 'Magic Sponge'. But Richard had plenty of experience with the injuries he had plus a broken leg he got playing as a student in the US, to give him first hand knowledge which has proved useful over the years.'

The end of Jane and Graham's time in the Coopers Arms came in 1998. The money that Jane and Graham had managed to save was primarily what they had made on making and serving food, but the brewery were looking to increase their fees to such an extent as to wipe out their small profits. It no longer made any sense financially. Jane recalls: 'When we came out of the pub we decided to just spend some time at the bungalow and enjoy not having any commitments. Apart from football games that is. We soon realised our money would not last so I went back to Bridgemere and Graham did gardening. A friend told him she knew of a lady requiring a gardener, Mrs Butcher. She asked Graham if he knew of anyone who could help with her housework, I went to see her and that was how it started. It fitted in well with my three or four days at Bridgemere.' Mrs Butcher became affectionately known as 'Mrs B' and Jane worked for her until she died in 2015. As well as cleaning, Jane effectively became a much-loved companion to Mrs B, to such an extent that she left her a generous bequeathal in her will. During this time Graham also worked carrying out stock-counts for WH Smith in various warehouses as well as a bit of gardening. Graham was always happy to work, although he would not be counting pencils for long. Football would soon get him back.

IF YOU MARRY A FOOTBALLER...

Graham with the European Cup at a football dinner, after Bob Paisley's Liverpool won it in 1981. Richard joined Manchester United in 2008 as a sports scientist and enjoyed being a part of the ultimate prize in club football that year, then the UEFA Champions League.

10 Old School, New School

1998 – 2008

As Graham's career came to a close in the nineties and noughties, son Richard's began. Where Graham started out at the coalface, playing for a top-flight club and ended in football's back office, namely at the Football League, Richard's career to an extent mirrored his Dad's, starting in the Football Association before working at West Bromwich Albion, Sheffield United and Manchester United. Richard's football career path is that of a sports scientist rather than player turned coach turned 'old wise head', still Graham's passion for the game as well as his core beliefs around how the game should be run, lives on through his younger son. Richard calls it 'old school', but what he really means by that is hard work, commitment, professionalism, zero interest in celebrity culture and more interest in a fulfilling, worthwhile career than earning the big bucks.

It was in the nineties that football changed forever and in a seismic way. Declining gate receipts in the eighties were replaced by big money TV rights for the bigger clubs and the gulf between the rich and poor was cemented in 1992 with the formation of the Premier League. The Premier League and its income from global TV deals has effectively transitioned top flight football clubs into world-wide brands, no longer reliant on the loyalty of local fans as evidenced by the calamitous attempt by a number of clubs to try and form a breakaway international 'Super-League' in 2021. Due to global exposure, players have also turned into brands, with many earning huge sums from sponsorship deals on top of eye-watering salaries from their clubs. For many, these giant clubs appear obscenely rich compared to lower league clubs struggling to survive on dwindling gates. In order to understand both Graham and Richard's roles at the English Football

League and Football Association respectively, somewhat in the shadow of their mighty Premier League partner, I think it's important to provide a little background as well as context as to where they fit in a post-Premier League world.

In the beginning there was the FA. The Football Association was founded in 1863 to resolve a rift between North and South, upper class and lower class. Its foundation created one set of rules for the game, where previously there had been two: the Sheffield Rules (the oldest football club being Sheffield FC - the connections just keep coming) and the Cambridge Rules, as determined by the University of Cambridge[33] (say no more). The FA Cup was established shortly afterwards. In 1885 The FA permitted professionalism and three years later came the Football League. Founded in 1888 with 12 clubs from the North and the Midlands, the Football League included many clubs with which Graham had strong connections: Blackburn Rovers, Preston North End, Stoke City and Wolverhampton Wanderers. Notably, the teams from the South, those which had followed the Cambridge rules and borne of the establishments of the likes of Eton and Harrow, were not part of it. Football became firmly established as a sport of the working classes.

In 1946, the English FA joined football's international governing body, FIFA, and the England team participated for the first time in the World Cup four years' later in 1950. By 1958, the English Football League (EFL) had grown to four leagues, representing 92 football clubs, 22 in Divisions One and Two, 24 in Divisions Three and Four. The battle lines were thus drawn between football's two governing bodies, the EFL and The FA - a dichotomy of club versus country, League Cup versus FA Cup. The tensions were most keenly felt at the top level of football, the old Division One, home to the country's best players who were most likely to compete in the national team as well as suffer from excessive fixture congestion for their clubs.

By the close of the eighties, football was in a bad way - declining gate receipts were compounded by organised mob violence by certain groups of football fans, a ban from competing in European competitions following the Heysel stadium disaster and an England team knocked out of the 1986 World Cup by Argentina, England's adversary in the Falklands War. The 1990 World Cup saw England go out on penalties to Germany, which whilst a bitter blow to national pride, was nonetheless a successful entertainment spectacle: over 25 million tuned in, representing the biggest sporting TV audience to date. Football as a business for media moguls had arrived, and would change the national game for ever with the creation of the Premier League in 1992. The FA approved the creation of the breakaway league of 22 clubs and facilitated the demise of the EFL into the poor relation. By way of comparison of the relative might of the now three governing bodies in football, the 2019 accounts (ie pre-COVID) of the Premier League report revenue of £3.2 billion, amounting to £160 million for each of the 20 clubs (reduced from 22 in the 1995/96 season) represented, whereas for the same period, the Football League had total revenue of £153 million, equalling just over £2 million for each of the 72 clubs they represent, a tiny fraction of that of the Premier League. The FA similarly has been dwarfed by the might of the Premier League, with revenues of £466 million in 2019, less than a sixth of that of the Premier League, to invest in the national game. It's hard not to ponder what our beautiful game would be today, had The FA had the foresight to push harder for a more equitable division of the TV spoils, a question many are seeking to unravel today. The formation of the Premier League (EPL) effectively created a new class divide funded by sponsorship; free from the shackles of responsibility towards football as a whole; the EPL has been a stupendous financial success and is now the most-watched sports league in the world. Top flight teams and their players generate global sponsorship revenues that dwarf amounts paid by fans to go and sit in the cold and support their team. Commercial activities at the bigger clubs dominate players' lives, and 'personalities' command premium transfer fees, leaving many to rue the roles of 'brand', 'lifestyle' and 'marketing' over football performances on the pitch.

The money swishing around the EPL clubs in the nineties attracted managers and players from far and wide and incredibly, since its inception, the EPL is still yet to be won by a team with an English manager. The last English manager to win the top English league was Howard Wilkinson, who took the Division One title with Leeds

United in 1991 and it was this man (also manager of the mighty Sheffield Wednesday from 1983 to 1988), whom The FA would appoint in January 1997 as technical director, tasked with modernising the English game and ultimately, generating players capable of winning the first trophy since 1966. Wilkinson published his vision, penned as the 'Charter for Quality' in May 1997, and it was the recommendations in this document, that would influence the latter years of Graham's career in football as well as the first years of son Richard's football career. The key message coming out of the Charter for Quality was that standards of coaching needed to improve in order to enable the English football team to compete at the highest level on a global stage. One area identified as needing investment was sports science, its importance increasingly recognised overseas as both protecting the health and well-being of young players as well as maximising performance. Howard Wilkinson wrote: 'The central figure in the recommendations for the 'Charter for Quality' is the player, and his or her best interests. Attempting to provide quality experiences for all young players at all levels is the overriding principle.'

Football may have changed in the nineties, but Graham still had his part to play. After many years of hard slog at the pub, Graham tried a few different jobs selling some pots, counting some pencils, a bit of gardening, but it wouldn't be long before an opportunity presented itself. Graham's first full-time role back in football was at Elite Sports (ESA) based in Oswestry, a company set up to deliver screening services including cardiac screening to professional sportsmen. In 1997, The FA began its compulsory cardiac screening programme of young elite football players, aiming to identify heart problems in young players, with a view to preventing fatal heart attacks on the football pitch. ESA were looking to get business from football clubs and Graham's network, football insight (and who knows, possibly even his experience as a pottery salesman) meant he was the perfect fit. He met Jon Pither, a physiologist who had previously worked in the army, at Elite Sports and the two formed a great friendship.

I asked Pither of his first impressions of Graham: 'Ooh look at that tan,' he replied, 'He was a big lump and always smiling, it was like an amber glow followed him down the corridor. Always smart.' It wasn't just Graham's natural good looks that impressed Pither though. ESA was a new company, run by successful businessmen and physicians, who not only wanted doors opening into football clubs, but also needed Graham to speak the language of football. Pither said of Graham: 'He listened intently and wanted to learn. He was aware of the issues around player well-being and could see how the services of ESA could help a player prevent injury and return safely to playing. He couldn't see how a hundred page document was going to be read by anyone at a football club and he was right. He managed to get all sorts of people to come and visit the centre. I would be tucked away in my little room and Graham would walk in with a household name of some sort and we would discuss heart screening. The very first player we had come to the centre for heart screening was a young Micah Richards. He was accompanied by the then Academy Director at Manchester City - Jim Cassell. Another friend of Graham's. I continued to do screening at Manchester City after ESA closed and Jim would always pop down to see me. This was echoed at many clubs - if Graham endorsed you and what you did and introduced you, it allowed us to work with them.' I asked Pither what clubs Graham was involved with: 'It would be easier to say which clubs he wasn't involved with really. He started with the clubs that he knew, which was basically every club. He seemed to know someone at every club or someone involved with that club, so getting to speak to the right people was quite easy with Graham around.'

Pither did have a number of funny stories to share, including a meeting with a Football Academy Director whom I won't name to spare blushes: 'We discussed cardiac screening, which he clearly pretended he understood and then we started explaining how our set up allowed us to send all the information that we would scan from the forms, a copy of the ECG and the echocardiogram via the internet to our cardiologist for reporting. He then looked at us both, swivelling his eyes between us, said nothing, but picked up the paperwork for the cardiac screening, rolled it up into a tube, waved it around in front of us and pointing at us with it, but saying nothing. After a few painful seconds all I said was: "What?". He flew into a bit of a rage to put it mildly, stood up, waving his arms about and shouting: "What do you take me for?", called us a pair of idiots and then said – and I remember this clear as day: "you expect me to believe that you can get these bits of paper into a cable and send them?!". At this point, you want to think someone is joking, but I knew he wasn't and I was just wondering how someone could be so out of touch, stupid. I am not sure what the word is. I remember looking at Graham and even he had a look on his face with his deeply frowning eyebrows and his mouth open, clearly thinking of something polite to say. Unfortunately I laughed, (in fact I am laughing now), that tipped ***** over the edge and he screamed at us to get out of his office! I hardly heard Graham swear, but he did after that. We got back to the car and you know when you laugh so hard you can't see properly, it was one of those moments. He also kept saying, "I am so sorry Jon, I am so embarrassed".' Funnily enough, Richard tells me this same character has the unlikely motto of 'Change or die'.

Graham was back in a world where he was comfortable, and whilst ESA didn't survive the DotCom bubble burst, closing just 18 months after it was launched, Pither set up another screening company (PML) with an ex-army colleague in 2006, which in 2021 conducts over half of the FA's cardiac screening. Despite their brief time together, the bonds of friendship between Pither and Graham endured; Graham and Jane went along to the opening of PML's first lab. Pither's closing words on Graham bely the deep impression he made: 'So thank you Graham for showing me and teaching me some important values. I am also quite proud to say that as a company we have never asked for anything of any club, we haven't bragged about what we do or who we screen. Some of Graham certainly rubbed off on me.'

A couple of years before the arrival of Howard Wilkinson at the FA, Richard was also looking into how science could protect the health of young footballers. He was completing his Masters in physiology and nutrition in Sports Science when he was asked if he would be interested in carrying out research into footballing injuries for a PhD. Dr Colin Fuller, from the Centre for Hazard and Risk Management department of Loughborough University, was interested in the application (or rather lack of it) of workplace health and safety legislation in the sports arena, and thought this was a useful area for further study in football. In 1995, legislation came into force requiring all employers (including football clubs) to systematically report injuries (RIDDOR - The Reporting of Injuries, Disease and Dangerous Occurrences Regulations), but most football clubs did not really have the systems or staff in place to properly implement it. Clubs would have professional physiotherapists, tasked with 'fixing' players when they broke down, but when Richard was completing his PhD in 1997, there was just one qualified sports scientist working in professional football in England - Dr Kunle Odetoyinbo (a contemporary of Richard's at Loughborough and a decent goalkeeper, by all accounts). Dr Fuller had hoped that The FA or the PFA would be interested in funding Richard's PhD - 'Injuries in professional football: identification of aetiological factors' - but no, ultimately Loughborough University footed the bill. Richard's former Manchester United colleague and Loughborough mate, Dr Tony Strudwick, in his book 'Soccer Science', hints that the reluctance to adopt sports science techniques by football clubs may be cultural and down to clubs resisting regulation by the footballing bodies: 'In 1958 The FA instituted courses for trainers on treatment of injury, although they were never compulsory. Even up to the 21st Century, clubs were reluctant to surrender control over whom they could employ and appointments were made through soccer's old boy network.'

One of the reasons The FA gave Richard for not providing funding for his PhD in 1994, was that they were about to conduct their own study. By 1997 Richard had completed his fieldwork - meticulously analysing hundreds of hours of football matches from the 1994 World Cup and 1996 Euros on videotapes, interviewing players and staff at four professional football clubs from the Midlands as well as seeking feedback from a number of other professional football clubs - and The FA got back in touch. They never did start their own study and please would Richard come and work for them and kick things off. Richard needed some persuading - he wanted a break from research - but his boss-to-be, Alan Hodson, a chartered physio, sold the role that would be Richard's first 'proper job'. Richard left his student house in Loughborough and moved back into the family home, Springbank, a 20 mile commute to The FA at Lilleshall.

OLD SCHOOL, NEW SCHOOL

Meanwhile, a year into his time at Elite Sports, Graham got a call from Jimmy Armfield[34], then working as a consultant for the Football League, to see if he was interested in a job in the Youth Development department, based in Preston. When Armfield died in 2018, the press recalled his time as a radio journalist when he was at a press conference held by Howard Wilkinson, then the beleaguered Sunderland's manager and getting a hard time. 'How many England caps have you got?' he asked the assembled media. From the back, the BBC radio pundit Armfield piped up. 'Forty-three, actually, Howard.' Nevertheless, there were no hard feelings between Wilkinson and Armfield and they shared many beliefs about what English football needed. Wilkinson's Charter for Quality recognised that it was within football clubs that future England players would be developed and coached, and that better coaching and standards were necessary: 'The FA is delighted that clubs wish to invest more time and money in the development of English players. These clubs should be encouraged... To maximise the potential of the best players in the country, it is, I believe, reasonable to allow more access to clubs who commit themselves employing the best possible coaches in the best facilities provided by themselves. I believe, however, that this access should only be available to those clubs who, under Football Academy Criteria, appreciably increase and improve their quality of provision.' In short, football clubs could have access to the time of talented young players as well as funding, provided they improved quality. Graham's role at the Football League would involve visiting clubs' Academies, advising on how they could improve as well as critically, determining whether or not they met the standards necessary to receive the considerable funding from the Football League. Or, as Richard described his Dad's role: 'Helping people who wanted to be helped.'

Jane recalls that whilst Graham enjoyed his role at Elite Sports, the opportunity Armfield described was a good one: 'The offer of a position at the Football League really appealed to Graham - exciting to be back in the world of football, yes too good to turn down and there was the security, pension and the perks of watching lots of football, all ages and levels.' Graham was still travelling a great deal and working hard, but nonetheless free of the weekly pressures of winning and losing football matches, free of the ever-present responsibility of managing the pub. It was a lifestyle they were both ready for. Jane remembers: 'Graham loved his footballing years - lots of ups and downs and excitement. Everything else after those years were always a close second. The Football League did give us many happy years. Lots of travelling though - approximately 36,000 miles a year. Many games to go to without the pressure of wanting a team to win. Graham was very content being back involved with teams and visiting the clubs he was responsible for, and watching the young boys develop their skills.'

It was at the Football League where Graham met Jim Briden, not a 'football man', but a 'money man' as Jane describes him, but who nonetheless became a great friend to both Jane and Graham and someone Graham respected a great deal. Briden told me: "I was working for Sport England and project managing the Lottery funded grant programme that was available to support EFL Academies, which required working closely with Graham and his colleagues. Graham then approached me to advise that there was a vacancy in the Youth Development department at the League, which he thought I would be ideal for. I was lucky enough to get the job, with as I later found out from my line manager, a strong recommendation from Graham.' Briden and Graham's friendship developed over many long car journeys, and Briden told me about their typical working week: 'He and I spent an awful lot of time on the road visiting EFL clubs, which would occupy at least four days of each week. We would also have to visit the office at least one day per fortnight, quite often to attend management meetings, which he was not overly keen on. He always said to me that he really could not be bothered with the politics (which are significant) associated with football, which I totally understood, but I don't think he appreciated how respected he was, because his opinion in such meetings was always valued. I think the part of the job he enjoyed the most was at weekends when he could simply go and watch Academy games and he would often have Jane for company (not sure how much she enjoyed those days out!!) before they (I mean he) analysed the games he had watched, over a spot of lunch.' Jane tells me she was happy to accompany Graham, and as a result has an intimate knowledge of the shopping centres all over the country (I believe Sheffield's Meadowhall was a favourite).

In trying to get to the bottom of what Graham did at the Football League, I came across a book by Chris Green from 2009, 'Every Boy's Dream: England's Football Future on the Line', a critique of England's failure to nurture its own talent and build a national team capable of winning big. Both Graham and Jim Briden feature heavily, described alongside Michael Tattershall (Deputy Operations Director) as: 'a holy trinity of Football League interviewees'. When I contacted Green, he remembered meeting Graham and in particular his compassion: 'I was touched by his response to a story I told him about a young boy whose life was detrimentally affected by his academy experience. Being a proper football person I think Graham got the depth of the story.' 'Every Boy's Dream' tells the tales of many English schoolboys who didn't make it as professional footballers and the brutal reality of the price of chasing a dream. Green had asked Graham about how young boys were treated when clubs told them they weren't going to make it: 'Graham Hawkins, the Football League's Head of Player Development, was aghast the word "culled" had been used but considered it a rare exception. "You do hear of one or two complaints," he said, "but I don't think that is typical".'

Briden also remembers meeting Green and reading his account of the experiences of young boys and their parents in the Academy system: 'One of the biggest challenges, as referenced in the book, is managing the expectations of the players and their parents. The professionalism and sometimes closeted nature of the Academy environment is such that the players almost expect that it will always be like that, so if and when they are released the disappointment is massive and sometimes difficult to deal with.' Graham talked about the ethos of the Academies in the early years to Green: 'It should be fun. We call that stage of development FUNdamental with the accent on the first three letters, and much of the practice isn't just about football, it's about ability, balance, coordination, speed (ABCs) and jumping.' When I shared this 'FUN' quote with Richard he laughed at how on-message his Dad was: 'That's straight out of The FA Youth Coach's manual!'

Green is critical of the inability of the Premier League, EFL and FA to co-ordinate youth football, but as Richard pointed out to me and as the revenue numbers bear out, The FA and the EFL just have no negotiating power as far as the Premier League is concerned. Briden recalls how Graham felt about the politics: 'One occasion that springs to mind and makes me laugh was when he walked out of a meeting in sheer frustration at the political nature of the debate. I recall him saying something along the lines of "I thought we were all here to help develop young players, but all we seem to be doing is creating obstacles to their development". It was so out of character as Graham was usually placid and very controlled, but on this occasion his passion and desire to make things better were overcome by sheer frustration.' Graham defended what the Football League were doing to develop young players, telling Green: 'We try to drive standards up. We pass on information and share good practice. There are many clubs with their own innovations, who are willing to share them, enabling the Football League to pass them on to other clubs. There are so many initiatives that have been integrated into the system you wouldn't recognise what goes on now compared to 11 years ago. We now have qualified physiotherapists, sports scientists, video technicians, sports psychologists, education officers and welfare officers. We are putting a lot of Continuing Professional Development (CPD) programmes together in an attempt to cover all these positions, now seen as essential in the development of the elite football player.'

I also came across a BBC blog by Paul Fletcher about exit trials, referencing Graham's role in them. Briden explained their importance: 'These were and still are a massive part of the EFL's exit strategy for players released by Academies. Initially only available to players released by Academies, due to Graham's sense of equality and fair play, the opportunity to attend these events was also extended to players released by Centres of Excellence (the level of operation below Academy but employed by the majority of EFL clubs) which meant that the number of players attending increased from about 40 to nearly 300. Despite the massive logistical challenges that this presented, Graham recognised the importance of giving the players that attended a second chance and as a result about 30 players each season received a scholarship offer after attending the trials, with a number then attaining professional contracts. Graham always coached one of the teams and his rapport with the players was obvious and his ability to make them feel at ease in very difficult and stressful circumstances was always evident.'

Football writer Paul Fletcher met Graham at these trials in February 2009, and his passion and commitment to all the young players was very much in evidence. Fletcher wrote: 'The trials cost around £15,000 to stage but I imagine that Hawkins, Briden and their team would try to put them on even if they cost a lot more. You can argue about the merits of youth systems and academy football, suggest that it is under-funded and not producing enough players, but the intention behind the exit trials must be applauded. I got a real sense that, for the Football League's Youth Development team, the boys were not products or a commodity but young people who had to be cared and looked after. In an era when football is a wealthy global business, people can be reduced to statistics, but the exit trials are an example of football's human face. As Hawkins said to me with great sincerity: "The care and welfare of the players is paramount".'

Whilst some of the narratives of 'Every Boy's Dream' of young boys who didn't make it can be harrowing, the improvement in the performance of the England team in the ten years since it was written can be evidenced by their place in the final of the 2020 Euros (held in 2021 due to Covid). I asked Briden if he thought we could in part thank him for that and he replied modestly 'I definitely think you can partly thank Graham! He had the foresight to appreciate that the way to improve the quality of young English players was to improve the standard of the coaching and increase the coaching contact hours that the players received.' When talking to Chris Green, Graham was confident that standards had improved during his time at the EFL: 'Go and talk to every one of the national team managers and they will say our players are good enough. The view nationally is that we're rubbish and technically deficient - but the national teams are getting better and winning games. It was in a mess ten years ago but now it couldn't be better. We have seen marked improvement in player development and we now need to give the players the opportunity to progress.'

Briden went on to explain more about Graham's contributions to football: 'The biggest positive of Graham's involvement with the

EFL was the experience, enthusiasm, positivity and respect that he brought to the organisation. This provided us with a platform to put forward our views on Youth Development and the Academy system as a whole and ensure that we had the support of our clubs when trying to introduce change. This was particularly evident in the initiatives that Graham was instrumental in developing such as the inclusion of festivals within the Academy games programme and a structured programme of CPD for all coaches that worked within the Academy system. Typically of Graham he was not satisfied with just affecting the areas in which he had experience (such as games and coaching), but through the knowledge and understanding that he gained from Richard and some of his colleagues (Tony Strudwick for example) in the area of Sports Science, he was able to develop the understanding and practices utilised within EFL Academies in this area. The opportunities that he was able to provide and 'champion' in this area made a massive difference to the physical testing and development programmes that Academies now deliver to players as part of their sports science programmes.'

At the time Graham was pushing the principles of the Charter for Quality in EFL clubs, Richard's work at The FA led to him designing and delivering training courses for all coaches; educating football clubs in managing the physical strain of playing football at the top level. In his book 'Soccer Science', Dr Tony Strudwick refers to his PhD supervisor, Professor Tom Reilly and his 1979 book, 'What Research Tells the Coach About Soccer', when explaining the role of sports science in football: 'The critical message from Reilly's findings was that soccer is an intermittent type of activity in which periods of short, high-intensity exercise are randomly interspersed with longer periods of either active rest or passive recovery. Training of soccer players should therefore be tailored accordingly. In addition, soccer players can be described as lean and muscular and having a reasonably high level in all areas of physical performance. That is, players need to be aerobically fit to run for long distances and anaerobically fit to produce bursts of power during the most intense phases of the game, especially during the later stages of the game when fatigue becomes more apparent. These findings were largely ignored by the English soccer establishment, where for generations of coaches, fitness was equated with the ability to run long distances.' In other words, preparing to play a season of football matches should be different to preparing to run a marathon in the Olympics, which seems remarkably obvious and simple, yet failed to be taken into consideration in the world of football until relatively recently. Richard made the connection with health and safety and sports science in his PhD: 'The ultimate aim of health and safety management is the elimination of accidents and ill health: in the case of professional football this would be equivalent to keeping all players fit, at all times, thereby allowing the club management to select from an injury free squad.' Clearly the players also benefit from 'following the science', which is designed to help them enjoy a long and healthy career. After Wilkinson's Charter for Quality, sports science became a compulsory element of The FA coaching courses and whilst at The FA, Richard delivered training to many household names in football management, including one Gareth Southgate, current England manager.

After many years of research, Richard's role at The FA was starting to feel like a training course production line. Although not actively looking for a role, when in February 2005 Richard got a call from Nigel Pearson, the time felt right for a move. Pearson, then assistant manager at Wolverhampton Wanderer's arch rival, West Bromwich Albion, invited Richard to come along to meet him and Manchester United legend and former England captain, Bryan Robson, West Brom's manager. Richard was ready to put his theories into practice, and enjoy some of the excitement of the highs and lows of being part of a football club. Robson and Pearson had both met Richard at FA coaching courses, and although they didn't know him well, thought he could be what they needed at West Brom. Robson was one of the first English managers to appreciate the role of sports science in football - Middlesborough is credited with creating the first sports science department in 1997 where he was player-manager from 1994 to 1997, and stayed on after retiring to coach them until 2001. Richard went on to work primarily with Pearson, whose own career had begun at Shrewsbury Town, expertly guided by none other than the then assistant manager Graham Hawkins.

A MARRIAGE MADE IN FOOTBALL

Richard's first season at the coalface would be one of the most memorable in West Brom's history and his three years there would be a baptism of fire into the highs and lows of football. Languishing at the bottom of the Premier League at Christmas 2004, West Brom were favourites to get relegated at the end of the season - indeed no club had ever survived if they were bottom at Christmas. In his autobiography, Robson describes the season that became known as 'The Great Escape': 'I said at the time that it was my greatest achievement and now, in the cold light of day, many months on, I still say the same. I won so many trophies at United and caps for England, but we were expected to have success at Old Trafford. That was normal. This was an achievement against the odds. At Albion, the expectation was to be relegated. The players were being written off as failures.' Despite the troubles, in February 2005, Richard arrived at a club with a fantastic atmosphere: 'They were just a really good bunch of lads,' he remembers, 'They were hard-working, no real egos, had a good relationship with each other, enjoyed their training and responded well to a new face coming in.' The results were good enough to give the players a chance of staying up if they won the final game of the season against Portsmouth, although that wouldn't have been enough - they needed other results to go their way.

Richard is typically modest about his contributions to that season: 'Well, I couldn't tell you if I made the players any fitter as I didn't test them. You can't really test in the middle of the season. Nigel was one of the best ones in that environment to keep the camaraderie going. The group of staff as a whole did that.' Robson references Richard in a couple of interviews, and in particular with reference to the team talk before that vital final match: 'People ask me what I said to the lads before that final game, against Portsmouth. In fact, we played them a six-minute video highlighting some of their best moments of that season – a great goal, tackle or save – and then left them to prepare themselves. And that was the idea of my coach, Nigel Pearson, as well as the fitness coach, Richard Hawkins.' Richard dug out the video for me, that the analyst had pulled together, and it's powerful, it's perfect. The soundtrack is a pre-match speech delivered by Al Pacino from the 1999 film, 'Any Given Sunday', to his American football team, accompanied by a soulful guitar. On the theme of 'inches' being the little things that add up to make the difference between winning and losing, the power of a team willing to go the extra mile for their team-mates. This is what Richard would call 'old school', but what I think he really means is that his Dad would have approved.

The following season at West Brom, the wheel of fortune did not spin in their favour. Richard remembers: 'We pretty much lost every game - it was tough. The hardest part was picking them up every Monday morning, but they were a great group, they were willing to work hard and I enjoyed the team spirit.' Unable to hang on, West Brom were duly relegated to the Championship in 2006. Robson left shortly after the start of the new season and was replaced by Tony Mowbray. Things were looking up in May 2007 when despite missing out on automatic promotion, a trip to the brand new Wembley Stadium beckoned for the play-off for the final spot in the Premier League. The match against Derby was dubbed 'the most lucrative game in world football in the world's most expensive stadium' and was only the second fixture held there - the first being The FA Cup Final (Chelsea beat Manchester United 1-0). Jane and Graham went along, but it wasn't the Baggies' day and they too lost 1-0. Jane remembers: 'We were waiting to see Richard before we left in one of the lounges and I could have cried when I saw his face, had never seen him look so disappointed. It was a long trip home.' At the Football League Graham was watching a lot of football, but without an allegiance to any club. With Richard at West Brom, that all changed and he and Jane shared the highs and lows with their son. Despite the fierce rivalry between Wolves and West Brom fans, any animosity Graham and Jane might have felt towards West Brom had evaporated when son Richard started work there.

Facing a second season in the Championship, Richard was starting to feel frustrated that he would be unable to further develop sports science at West Brom and when requests for investment were turned down, he began to look around for his next role. A couple of opportunities presented themselves at the same time: Robson came calling when he took up a new role at Sheffield United in September 2007 as did Rob Swire, a physio at Manchester United under the legendary Sir Alex Ferguson. A chat with Robson's assistant, Brian Kidd went well and a move was secured. Nevertheless, the chance to build a department at Manchester United was incredibly exciting and Richard anxiously awaited news. The call from Sir Alex came whilst he was at a pre-season race day with West Brom, telling him: 'We've gone with the boy Strudwick.' It was disappointing, but Richard acknowledges his friend Tony was the better fit: 'He had so much more experience in clubs than I did at that time.'

Nevertheless, Richard didn't have to wait long before Manchester United would come calling again: Ferguson had recruited Strudwick to build a sports science department and 'Struds' wanted Richard to be part of it. This time Richard would turn them down, albeit briefly. Richard explained: 'I'd just started a new job and whilst I very much wanted to go and work at Manchester United, I told them I would have to wait until the end of the season as I owed it to Bryan.' Just a couple of weeks later, in January 2008, after losing to Sheffield Wednesday, Sheffield United fans were calling for Robson's head. By February, after another South Yorkshire derby against 10-man Scunthorpe, a goal-less draw, the fans were incensed with hundreds of them waiting around for an hour and a half after the match threatening to lynch the manager. Richard remembers the scenes, fearing for his and the manager's safety, leaving the ground many hours after the end of the game under a police escort. Robson and Sheffield United parted ways shortly afterwards and Richard felt free to leave. Where he'd had to serve ten weeks notice at West Brom, a call from Ferguson to Sheffield United's chairman meant he was forthwith on his way across the Pennines to start his new job. 14 years later and Richard is still at Manchester United. Jane and Graham enjoyed many trips to Old Trafford, catching up with Richard afterwards. Jane remembers: 'We both loved going to Man Utd, and the bonus was seeing Richard after the game. Graham would often bump into football people he knew, but don't ask me who. The trip to Rome was really special (shame we lost).' The 'trip to Rome' was the Champions League Final in 2009 where Manchester United lost to Barcelona. Jane uses 'we' to refer to Manchester United, as she did for whichever team Graham or Richard were working for. 'I do remember when we first went to see Wolves play against Manchester United and before the game, Graham said he wasn't sure who he would be supporting,' Jane recalls, 'As soon as we sat down though, he looked at me and said: "I know who I'm supporting" and that was that.' Despite family coming before any club allegiance, Wolves always remained a big part of Graham's life and he went regularly to Molineux as well as Old Trafford. 'Always managed to get tickets for Wolves through the guys at the Academy,' Jane remembers.

Graham was incredibly proud of his family, and everyone I spoke to echoed how much his wife Jane, sons Ian and Richard and granddaughters Lauren, Amy, Holly and Louisa meant to him. Both Ian and Richard enjoyed playing football as boys, and indeed both had talent, but there was never any expectation or particular desire that either of them should follow in Graham's footsteps. Jane and Graham were just happy for their boys to follow their own dreams, being on hand for advice when called upon, but never ones to push them in any one direction. I asked Richard several times if his Dad's extensive football network ever helped him out in his own career and he just looked at me like I was asking a stupid question. Graham knew Nigel Pearson, but it was training courses that Richard had delivered whilst at The FA that had brought him to the attention of both Bryan Robson and Pearson. Whilst at the EFL, Graham had attended some of Richard's coaching courses on sports science. Neither let on that they knew each other and it was only afterwards that others in the room with Graham made the connection from the surnames. Jane told me Graham's silence was deliberate as he enjoyed listening with pride to his football colleagues make positive remarks about Richard's sessions without knowing it was his son.

Graham retired in March 2011, aged 65, and he stopped getting paid for watching football. Clearly, he carried on watching football, a lot of football, but there was more time for the greatest loves of his life, his wife, sons and granddaughters. Springbank, the bungalow just outside Woore that had almost bankrupted them in 1984, came into its own as the place where the four girls would be together, playing in the huge garden or as they got older, choreographing dance videos. Retirement also enabled Jane and Graham to go on many holidays together, in some respects making up for the times they had been unable to go due to football or pub commitments. It wasn't all dance shows and holidays though; in August 2009 Graham was diagnosed with non-Hodgkin Lymphoma, a cancer that starts in the body's white blood cells, the heart of the body's immune system. It was a devastating blow: Jane, Graham, Ian and Richard would never really know how long Graham would have left, although one thing was certain - each of them would do their utmost to cherish those last years.

OLD SCHOOL, NEW SCHOOL

Jane and Graham celebrating their 60th birthdays at Molineux with their precious granddaughters. Girls from L to R: Lauren, Louisa, Holly, Amy.

11 The Big 'C' is for Charity and Chicken

2008 – 2016

The Birmingham Mail interviewed Graham in 2012, as Graham publicised one of his fundraising events at Molineux and led with the headline: 'Former Wolves boss Graham Hawkins: my cancer will kill me but until then I'll take each day at a time.' The original cancer diagnosis had come some three years previously, in August 2009. Jane explains: 'He went to see a specialist re a hernia and the specialist he saw found the lump under the diaphragm. Then followed loads of tests and a meeting with Dr. O'Connor at the Royal Shrewsbury Hospital. Very difficult time, hard to take it all in.' Graham was just 63. Graham explained his diagnosis to the Birmingham Mail: 'I've got what they call low grade non-Hodgkin lymphoma, which is a kind of leukaemia that doesn't go away. I have scans regularly. My next one is in April, so things are going alright at the moment. I've had the chemotherapy but the specialist has said he doesn't think it will go away – they normally don't. He said hopefully it will keep away for five or six years, but then I'll need more treatment. I've had stem cells frozen and they're kept at Birmingham's Queen Elizabeth Hospital. That's the next throw of the dice really. But chemotherapy and a blood transfusion will give me five, six, seven or eight... however many more years.'

Uncle David remembers spending a lot of time with Graham during treatment and confronting gruelling processes with typical stoicism and good humour: 'When he first went in there, the Queen Elizabeth, he was in a room on his own. I went to visit on a Sunday, I'd taken him some hair clippers. There was a food chart to fill

THE BIG 'C' IS FOR CHARITY AND CHICKEN

in and one of the nurses was coming round to get it. Of course me having no hair you see, the nurse thought I was the patient. Graham shouted out from the bathroom "put down whatever, 'cause you'll eat it anyway"!'

Despite this gentle ribbing of his brother-in-law, after his diagnosis Graham was taking food seriously. As a sports scientist, Richard had always had an interest in the the role nutrition played in performance, and after receiving the devastating news of his father's diagnosis, he was keen to share what he knew with his parents. 'There was a lot of research out there that suggested that cutting back on sugar could help with cancer treatment,' says Richard. Jane remembers: 'Some of the chemo did affect the taste buds so food he always loved tasted so different to what he remembered. He never had much of a sweet tooth so it was quite easy for him to reduce sugar.'

It wasn't the first time Graham had made radical changes to his diet; one summer in the early nineties he decided he wanted to become a vegetarian. Their bungalow just outside Woore neighboured farmland where Graham and Jane looked out on fields of frolicking newborn lambs and calves in the spring, and he'd often toyed with the idea of giving up meat. Jane explains: 'Graham had been to Newcastle and on the way back drove behind a slaughterhouse lorry with legs sticking out of the sides. For him, that was the final straw. Problem was Ian was getting married and he'd ordered chicken for the wedding. I persuaded him to continue eating chicken, then after the wedding he went pescatarian.' Jon Pither, with whom Graham worked at Elite Sports and had spent ten years in the army could not equate vegetarianism with the former footballer: 'I refused to believe he was a vegetarian and would tease him about what he had brought in for lunch.' Many of my student peers became vegetarians in the early nineties, yes, mostly female, but being a middle-aged man wasn't going to stop Graham doing something he believed in. Similarly, son Ian, possibly remorseful of making his Dad eat chicken at his wedding (!) became vegan in his 40s. After reading Lance Armstrong's 2000 book, 'It's Not About the Bike' (many years before he was outed as a drugs cheat in 2012) in which he extolled the virtues of eating chicken to help repair his body whilst undergoing cancer treatment, Graham went back to eating poultry, which the interweb informs me, made him a 'pesce-pollotarian'.

Jane explained the treatment Graham underwent after the initial diagnosis: 'A week of CT scans, a biopsy of tissue and a biopsy of bone marrow. Then tablet form chemo, tiny tablets 20 at a time for three days then again in three weeks. The middle week was always stay clear of others as his immune system was very low. This was for three months. The next lot of chemo was January 2011 for five months, again every three weeks. The final chemo was January 2016 prior to having stem cells replaced at Queen Elizabeth Hospital in Birmingham.' Much of the treatment involved a lot of sitting around and waiting - something both Jane and Graham found difficult. Whilst Graham was still working for the EFL for 18 months after his initial diagnosis, after he retired, both he and Jane threw themselves into raising money for various charities. This was not something that was new to them - both Graham and Jane had been involved in charity work back when they had moved to Woore in 1978. Many choose to blast footballers for getting involved in charitable causes, diminishing their efforts with blasé throw-away remarks referring to how easy it is for them, how they are so wealthy it is their prerogative to give something back. In truth, footballers' involvement in fund-raising to help others has very little to do with wealth and a lot more to do with the platform afforded to them by the fans. As a former player and manager with a massive football network, Graham had spent much of his career serving tens of thousands of fans on a Saturday afternoon, who loved the game from afar. In simple economics, he was well-placed to leverage his network to raise money for good causes. For Jane, charity fund-raising became part of her DNA, part of being involved in the communities she lived in whilst supporting Graham - part of being married to football. Still today, she is as active as ever in local fund-raising communities, organising raffles, music nights, sitting on committees, making cakes and giving her time and energy to help others.

One particularly memorable charity event took place just before Graham's second season at Shrewsbury kicked off. In July 1981, the world watched the royal wedding of the 32 year old heir to the throne, Prince Charles, to 20 year old Lady Diana Spencer. The people of Woore loved to stage an event, and everyone was out socialising together. 'It was a wonderful day,' said Jane. There were competitions, a footy tournament in the morning, then a picnic lunch all on the cricket club field, followed later with a disco in the village hall. The fancy dress competition was won by the 'wedding party', with ten-year old Ian as the bride in Jane's wedding dress, eight-year old Richard and friend as bridesmaids wearing dresses that Jane had worn at Wolverhampton friends Jenny and Margaret's weddings, and another schoolfriend was the groom, with gold braid stitched around his school blazer. 'They wore wigs and looked so good that the judge thought they were girls - so they lifted their skirts to reveal footy shorts socks and trainers ready to play in a five-a-side.' It was around this time that the Woore Variety Artists was founded - Jane explains: 'Anyone who felt they had anything to offer was asked to come to a meeting, actually there were a fair amount of good singers and actors plus a variety of entertainment. It was an enormous success and went on for four evenings and was held every year for about 20 years raising thousands for a selection of charities.' Tickets were sold to the Woore Variety Artists' annual event, to friends and family who came for a good night out. They were held in the Woore Victory Hall, a 1950s building in the centre of the village. Everyone pitched in, even reluctant performers Graham and Jane. Richard remembers his Dad gamely performing Edelweiss and his Mum getting dressed up for a dance routine. The group included professional musician Ken Warrilow - still performing today with his sons and still involved in charity fund-raising with Jane.

Much of the Woore fund-raising activities centred around the Coopers Arms, and when Jane and Graham became landlords, held many events over the years to raise money for charity. Graham's footballing connections also came to lend their support as Jane recalls: 'Woore Variety Artists raised thousands for a selection of charities and as they were held in the pub, we didn't have to pay for a venue. We usually held pie and pea suppers. Our suppliers would give good discounts on produce. Stanley Matthews and Eddie Clamp[35] (Stoke and Wolves respectively) came to push over the pile of pennies (actually twopence) one time. We always had raffles with donated prizes.' Wherever Jane and Graham went, they would invariably pitch in with charitable events and in Bahrain, this stretched the reluctant athlete Jane to do a leg of a marathon relay alongside Graham and the boys.

It was almost inevitable, therefore, that after Graham's cancer diagnosis the pair would use their experiences to try and help others going through similar tough times. Graham spent hours sitting around getting treatment and entertained himself with his iPad, and felt for fellow patients in the unit who didn't have access to such technology. The first iPad was launched in 2010, and so was brand new technology at the time and unaffordable for many patients. He told Birmingham Mail journalist, Mat Kendrick in 2012 about how he got his old boss Graham Turner involved: 'I was having my chemotherapy and I thought: "If I get out of this okay there's got to be something I can do to raise a little bit of money to make the next patient's life easier". I went to Graham with the idea of doing a dinner at Shrewsbury and probably one at Molineux as well. He said "Great", and we could split the money between Shrewsbury and Wolverhampton Hospitals. I said I was reluctant to pay a speaker and asked him if he fancied doing it – so that's exactly what we've done.'

Mat Kendrick reported that Wolves icons John Richards, Geoff Palmer[36], Dave Wagstaffe[37], Mike Bailey[38], Wayne Clarke[39], Ron Flowers[40], Gerry Harris[41], John McAlle[42], Willie Carr[43], Keith Downing[44] and Fred Kemp[45] were all at the fundraiser at Molineux, with Graham commenting: 'The lads have been great, to be fair, and Wolves have been superb as well. Everyone has been very helpful.' Ian and Richard also came along, reminiscing about their time as ball boys there.

Even though Graham's cancer treatment was draining, he was determined to make every second count and ultimately enjoyed over six years of retirement. He and Jane went on numerous holidays, sometimes just the two of them, sometimes with Richard, Ian and the granddaughters. Graham followed Richard's career at Manchester United with interest, taking Jane whenever Richard could get tickets. In August 2015, when I met Richard on our first date, he talked a lot about his Dad and how he would be getting his stem cell treatment in the spring of 2016 and how he hoped it would give him a new lease of life. His parents' wedding anniversary was coming up, as was their 70th birthdays and Richard organised a big family get-together in a house in the Cotswolds over a long weekend. It would be the last big family event with Graham present.

No one knew that September 2016 would be the final goodbye, but in the months leading up to that moment, the family was nonetheless readying itself. One of Graham's final acts of love for his beloved wife was to ensure that she was safely installed in a new house in the village of Eccleshall. The bungalow's three-quarters of an acre garden had been perfect for family gatherings in summers home from Bahrain and for the four granddaughters to explore together, but too much for a septuagenarian lady to manage on her own. After some delays in the chain, Jane and Graham rented a small house in Eccleshall whilst they waited for the vendors of their new house to move out. Graham would never live there - Jane would move house alone just days after losing her husband. For many, dealing with a house move in the days before Graham's funeral would have been too much, but it didn't phase Jane - possibly it was a comfort to find herself housed where Graham had wanted her to feel safe, as well as a distraction from thinking too much.

Jane, Ian and Richard were all with Graham when the time came, some seven years after the cancer diagnosis. 'The worst news,' Richard's text message to me read. In a hospital bed, surrounded by medical equipment and the whiff of antiseptic, Graham's iPad was playing 'Human' by the Killers. It all happened so quickly and in the end it was pneumonia that got the better of Graham. Stem cell treatment from the spring had left Graham's immune system vulnerable, and whilst he'd been active, even playing tennis over the summer, there was a chink in his armour that was viciously exploited by infection. It was too soon for everyone, everyone wanted more years with him, and yet it was a life well lived, full of love. The dancer in the Killers' song has been interpreted by some as a puppet, one who dances to someone else's tune. Graham learned to be a dancer to impress his Jane, he danced for a while on the pitch but remained

A MARRIAGE MADE IN FOOTBALL

proudly his own man, charting his course through a life in football, always with Jane by his side.

THE BIG 'C' IS FOR CHARITY AND CHICKEN

Raising money for charity took many forms for Graham and Jane - here getting involved with the Woore Variety Artists.

Afterword

After meeting Graham just the one time, three months later I found myself at his funeral alongside hundreds of people I didn't know. I was one of the ones standing at the back, under the kindly watch of Uncle David and his wife Angela who'd had their brief to look after me, whilst my boyfriend read his eulogy. I'd encouraged Richard to speak and share his stories. I thought it would help him grieve. I'd first realised the magical, healing power of words to make sense of the loss of a loved one back in 2006, when I'd attended the funeral of the little sister of my good friend and talented writer, Boris Starling. Belinda had died suddenly aged just 34, leaving behind a husband and two young children. Boris' words on that day are etched in my memory. I was awed by his courage to stand up in front of hundreds of mourners, to tell stories that would help others find meaning in the wake of an immense loss. My mother's funeral in 2012 was the first time I'd had the courage to share my own words with an audience, also in the form of a eulogy.

Graham and Jane's marriage was a happy one and their love story an uncomplicated one, but no less powerful for its simplicity. Graham touched so many people's lives through football, but I believe that he would say that his ability to make some of the bolder decisions in life came from the strength he took from Jane's unwavering belief in and devotion to her husband. Those decisions led to some of their most rewarding experiences, exciting adventures and ultimately a rich life well-lived. It's been an honour and a privilege to write Graham and Jane's story, somewhat akin to a DIY 'Who Do Think You Are' project. My own Marriage Made in Football is in its infancy, though now we're both 50, we're well into the second half of life, but looking forward to whatever adventures that may bring. I have learned many things during this process, but as far as marrying into football goes, I'd recommend embracing it, welcoming the game into your life as you

AFTERWORD

would a child. Football may be capricious, it will bring joy and worry in equal measure, but overall it's a rollercoaster well worth the ride.

***

A MARRIAGE MADE IN FOOTBALL

Dress as you were in the sixties for Jane and Graham's 25th wedding anniversary celebration in the Coopers Arms. Always game, Ian came dressed as a baby.

Eulogy

Richard Hawkins, October 2016

My Dad would be so proud of seeing you all here today. I would just like to start by introducing myself as Jane and Graham's younger son Richard, and I am honoured to be able to stand here and hopefully, with the help given to me from my Mum and brother Ian, the next few minutes will portray my Dad as the great man we all knew and loved.

I'll start at the beginning. Born 5th March 1946, at a whopping 12 pounds! With feet that size he was destined for a career in football. Football obviously played a major part in his life and many of the characteristics that were evident in his professional career clearly served him well throughout his life.

Dad grew up with his two sisters, Susan and Maureen, and younger brother Andrew. Unfortunately Dad missed the opportunity of having an older brother as sadly Ernie died before he was born.

Dad was fortunate to begin his footballing career at the club he had supported from the terraces. At 16 he faced new challenges both on and off the field, those off it potentially being the most daunting; having recently met my Mum he sought out some dancing tuition from an old girlfriend – this was obviously time well spent, as he must have made the right moves on the dance floor – you could say he had pretty good feet both on and off the pitch!

Dad was fortunate enough to travel the world with his job and made so many friendships along the way, evident of what I see before me. Football has moved on with so many changes taking place over the past few decades compared to my Dad's generation, however it was during his time at Blackburn that I first experienced the strength of the bonds that existed between players and families. The warm atmosphere of the players' lounge after games, the mixing of players and fans in the 100 Club, and the family holidays down in Cornwall staying in a B&B above Joe Mercer's pub – it seemed like half the team were there enjoying their summer holidays, far removed from the private residences on remote islands that players enjoy today.

One of the few regrets I have is not really seeing much of my Dad play. Even though my Mum religiously took Ian and I to every home game, I was usually asleep by half-time – no reflection on the entertainment I am sure! It was during his time at Wolves as manager that I began to take more notice, although I am not sure whether my Mum appreciated it. It was the 1982/83 promotion season that Ian and I became ball boys at Molineux. Someone decided to park us either side of the dugout to curb my Dad's language during the game - I can see the shock on your faces, as many of you would never have heard him swear. All was good the first year but the second season wasn't successful; there was a lot of swearing!

As one door closed another opened, and it was following my Dad's departure from Wolves that our Middle Eastern adventure began – without doubt the best family experience we ever had. Fantastic lifelong friendships were made, a new culture experienced and if you were sporty and liked the sun it was paradise. There are so many fond memories of my Dad during this time but I want to share three, which I am sure he enjoyed. Christmas time in football is a busy period. Who would have thought though having spent the previous 22 years working on Christmas Day and preparing for a Boxing Day game that as a family we would be able to spend it on the Sheikh's Beach. Christmas 1984, our first Christmas Day in Bahrain spent on the beach with a bit of keepy-uppy and windsurfing – I can't remember any of us being any good (at windsurfing that is).

A second memory is the Bahrain marathon relay. My Dad, Ian and myself were able to run in the same team together, Ian handing over the baton to Dad and then Dad to me. A great event with other members of the team here today. Some of you may be wondering about my Mum... she did do a three kilometre stage one year, but generally played the role of faithful supporter in everything my Dad did.

The third memory takes us back to football, and was no doubt a proud moment for my Dad when he first played in the same team as Ian and I for The British Club in the Bahraini Expat League. I can't remember who played where but as long as my Dad had young legs around him he would always be able to find the right pass, with his left or right; I still don't know another player who was left-footed but took penalties with his right!

The Bahrain experience came to an end in 1990 and a new chapter began. I certainly enjoyed the period during which my parents played landlord and landlady at the Coopers Arms. Myself a university student at the time, took full advantage of my newly acquired taste for alcohol!

During their time at the pub my parents adopted three dogs, Dad being the instigator, a big softie really. Each appeared in the village by some means and ended up at the pub. Ben, Blossom and Hector were all faithful companions with Hector following Dad's every move, effectively being his shadow.

It was during those six years that my Dad began his drive to support as many charities as he could. Typical of him though, through all his endeavours he never sought any accolades for his work, and was always happy to fly under the radar.

Dad had a variety of roles in professional football over the years and he always expressed his passion for nurturing young football talent and getting the best out of them. Even during his time coaching at Shrewsbury and managing Wolves, he found the time to coach the local boys team; myself nine and Ian 11 at the time, still have friends that remind us of those fun years. Later in his career he continued with this passion, showing his commitment and appetite through his endeavours in youth development whilst working for the Football League.

Throughout his life he has always had a love of music and live entertainment, initiated no doubt by those early days on the dance floor with my Mum. From major acts and West End shows to amateur productions he enjoyed them all, and often spoke fondly of the great nights he had had and the fantastic people he shared them with.

Dad extended his charity events into retirement and the past five years have been consumed with his contributions to Cancer Research as well as having as many holidays as possible with Mum, and enjoying as much time as possible with his four gorgeous granddaughters. I think he took more pride in these four girls than he did in any other aspects of his life and I have no doubts that all four, Lauren, Amy, Holly and Louisa, will fulfil their dreams for him. The four often debated which one of them was Granddad's favourite – I think that debate will continue for some time!

I see my Dad in a different light now, but I guess that is inevitable. It is evident to me that he touched so many people and I am so pleased to see everyone here today from all aspects of his life.

He was a leader, a true gentleman, loyal and considerate. He could also hold an audience and tell a good story once he got going, however I am sure there are lots more I never got to hear (that's what this afternoon is for). He epitomised the term professionalism and was someone you could always count on, someone you all called your friend.

Here, we remember his life. Later though, we want to celebrate his life. Yes, we are sad, distraught, devastated, but we must celebrate the life he had and the friendships he brought together.

I would like to finish by reading the last page of a book recently published by Edward Skingsley. The book is an account of the 1970/71 Championship winning season at Preston North End.

EULOGY

'The book was just about finished but I needed a Foreword to make it complete. After plucking up enough courage I contacted Graham and ran the idea past him. That led to a meeting that lasted some three hours, where he shared with me, not only his special memories of that North End season, but of his whole life in football. He has done an awful lot in the game. It was bliss. The stories were just wonderful, as was his company that day. What does come shining through about Graham though is his modesty. I'm not quite sure if he believed me when I said I always mentally compare any subsequent North End defence with that of 1970/71, and always find myself leaning towards the one he led so admirably back then. I had already written in my squad biography notes that I regard him as a 'colossus' of that North End team. However, I would like to add he is a 'colossus' of a gentleman too.'

Bibliography

The British Newspaper Archive: thousands upon thousands of contemporary newspaper articles. My favourite find has to be Ernie Hunt's sixties light-hearted, upbeat weekly column on Wolves' dressing room gossip and banter, which was subsequently taken over by his team-mate and Wolves captain, Mike Bailey.

Clive Corbett, Those Were The Days: A History of Wolverhampton Wanderers 1964-77 (Geoffrey Publications, 2007)

Clive Corbett, Out of Darkness: A History of Wolverhampton Wanderers 1977-90 (Geoffrey Publications, 2011)

David Harrison and Steve Gordos, The Doog: The Incredible Story of Derek Dougan, Football's Most Controversial Figure (Know The Score Books, 2008)

David Tossell, In Sunshine or in Shadow - A Journey Through the Life of Derek Dougan (Pitch Publishing Ltd, 2012)

John Burridge, Budgie: The Autobiography of Goalkeeping Legend John Burridge (John Blake, 2015)

David Instone, Wolves All Over the World (Thomas Publications, 2015)

Edward Skingsley, A Season to Savour: Preston North End 1970/71 (Create Space Independent Publishing Platform, 2016)

Edward Skingsley, Preston North End: The Sixties (Create Space Independent Publishing Platform, 2016)

BIBLIOGRAPHY

Edward Skingsley, Preston North End: The Seventies (Independently published, 2018)

Harry Berry, Blackburn, A Century of Soccer: 1875 - 1975 (the Club, 1975)

Mike Jackman, Blackburn Rovers: The Complete Record 1875 - 2009 (DB Publishing, 2014)

Jeff Kent, The Valiants' Years: Story of Port Vale (Witan Books, 1990)

Mike Jones, Breathe on 'em Salop: Official History of Shrewsbury Town FC (Yore Publications, 1995)

Martin Knight and Dave Mackay, The Real Mackay: The Dave Mackay Story (Mainstream Publishing, 2005)

Dr Richard Hawkins, Injuries in Professional Football. Identification of Aetiological Factors (Badminton Press, 1997)

Dr Tony Strudwick, Soccer Science (Human Kinetics Australia PL, 2016)

Michael Calvin, The Nowhere Men: The Unknown Story of Football's True Talent Spotters (Arrow, 2014)

Chris Green, Every Boy's Dream: England's Football Future on the Line (A&C Black Publishers Ltd, 2009)

Bryan Robson, Robbo: My Autobiography (Hodder & Stoughton, 2006)

Tributes

Football colleagues lost during the writing of this book

George McAllister (Bahrain physio)
Died aged 72, May 2020

Gerry Harris (Wolves left-back in Cullis era)
Died aged 84, July 2020

Fred Davies (team-mate at Wolves)
Died aged 81, Sept 2020

Nobby Stiles (team-mate at Preston)
Died aged 78, Oct 2020
Diagnosed with dementia

Ron Flowers (team-mate at Wolves)
Died aged 87, Nov 2021

Gordon Lee (manager at Blackburn)
Died aged 87, March 2022

TRIBUTES

Football colleagues impacted by dementia

Dave Mackay (football colleague in the Middle East)
Died 2015

Neil Wilkinson (team-mate at Blackburn)
Died 2016
Diagnosed with Pick's disease in early 50s

Ernie Hunt (team-mate at Wolves)
Died June 2018
Suffered from Alzheimer's disease

Stan Cullis (legendary manager of Wolverhampton Wanderers)
Died 2001

Tony Parkes (team-mate at Blackburn)
Family shared diagnosis of Alzheimer's disease Feb 2020

Mike Bailey (team-mate at Wolves)
Family shared diagnosis Nov 2020

Bobby Charlton (manager at Preston)
Diagnosis reported Nov 2020

Apologies as the above lists are bound to be incomplete; illustrative rather than exhaustive.

Notes

[1] Fred Davies was the first-team goalkeeper at Wolverhampton Wanderers in the sixties. Went on to manage Shrewsbury Town 1993-1997.

[2] Bob is Jane's brother, Robert.

[3] Alan Bloor: centre half at Stoke City 1960-78, out with a calf injury in the summer of 1969 and so Graham took his spot on in the England 'A' team tour. Both men would go on to coach together at Port Vale.

[4] Angela Turner, wife to Jane's brother David.

[5] Whelan went on to be a successful retailer, owning JJB Sports, the second largest sports retailer in the eighties and nineties and bought Wigan Athletic in 1995.

[6] 'Blackburn, A Century of Soccer: 1875-1975', Harry Berry

[7] Roger Jones, Blackburn goalkeeper 1970-76.

[8] Bryan Douglas - 438 caps for Blackburn, 1952-69, 100 goals.

[9] John Richards - played striker both with and under Graham at Wolves, in a career lasting from 1969-1983, scoring 194 goals. Became director of Wolves in 1994, managing director 1997-2000.

[10] Adrian Heath: Stoke youth player who went on to sign for Everton in 1982 for a then record signing fee for the club of £750,000.

[11] Lee Chapman: Stoke youth player who scored 79 goals for Sheffield Wednesday in 186 appearances between 1984-88 and was my childhood footballing hero (nothing to do with rugged good looks).

[12] Nigel Pearson played for Sheffield Wednesday 1987 - 1994 and was Man of the Match in the Owls' 1991 League Cup Victory over Manchester United at Wembley. He has been a football manager since 1998, managing both Leicester and Watford in the Premier League, currently managing Bristol City in the Championship.

[13] 'In Sunshine or in Shadow - A Journey Through the Life of Derek Dougan' by David Tossell.

[14] 'The Doog - The Incredible Story of Derek Dougan: Football's Most Controversial Figure' by David Harrison and Steve Gordos.

[15] Sir Jack Hayward went on to become Wolves' owner in 1990, investing considerable sums to support his team back to their former glory.

[16] Teletext was pages of text you could access on the telly - a precursor to news on the internet. The ITV version was called ORACLE, BBC version was Ceefax, and had content such as news headlines, weather and TV guides.

[17] Stewart Ross had played for Wolves alongside Derek Dougan and Graham, making his debut in 1968 against Manchester United. He trained as an accountant after retiring from football and he and Graham remained good friends after their time together at Wolves in the eighties, with Ross acting as the Hawkins' accountant when they ran the Coopers Arms pub.

[18] See Chapter Nine, 'If You Marry a Footballer…'.

[19] See Chapter Eight, 'From Woore to War and Back Again'.

[20] By 'canned stuff' Dougan means edited highlights as offered by Match of the Day at the time.

[21] In October 1981 Bryan Robson became the country's most expensive player at £1.5m, beating the previous record held by Wolves' Andy Gray in September 1979 of £1,469,000.

[22] Kenny Hibbitt: Wolves legend, 544 appearances 1968-84. Experienced player under Graham's tenure as manager.

[23] Bill Nicholson was Spurs manager 1958-74.

[24] George McAllister, physio to Bahraini National Team.

[25] One of several private members' clubs, made up largely of ex-pats, with pool, sports facilities, restaurant and bar.

[26] Dave Mackay was a Scottish footballing legend, part of the Tottenham side that won both the league and FA Cup in 1961, Mackay went on to win the league as a manager of Derby County in 1975.

[27] Mick Mills was full back at Ipswich Town as well as Southampton and Stoke City, playing for England 42 times between 1972-82.

[28] The requirement to upgrade all stadia to all-seaters was subsequently relaxed in 1992 to apply only to the top two leagues.

[29] Rubery Owens - British engineering company founded in Darlaston in 1884. The main Darlaston site closed in 1981.

[30] Jake King played as a full back for Shrewsbury Town from 1971-82, making over 300 appearances.

[31] Javea is a small holiday resort in the province of Alicante, Spain, where Maree and Macca, Jane and Graham's friends from Bahrain, have lived for many years.

[32] Sir Stanley Matthews, Stoke City and England footballing legend. Like Graham, he had a brief spell as a manager at Port Vale (1967-68) and it did not go well.

[33] Cambridge University (Trinity College) is my alma mater.

[34] Jimmy Armfield was a member of England's World-Cup winning football squad 1966, right-back at Blackpool 1954-1971 and manager of England 'A' team when Graham went on tour with them in 1969.

[35] Eddie Clamp's mother, 'Mrs Clamp', was the fearsome matriarch responsible for kit-washing at Wolves back in the sixties. Derek Dougan brought Mrs Clamp back to Wolves in the eighties.

[36] Geoff Palmer: right-back for Wolves 1971-84, 1985-86, one of Graham's more experienced players when he was manager. Became a policeman when he retired from football.

[37] Dave Wagstaffe: 'Waggy', left-winger, played at Wolves and Blackburn with Graham. Died of a heart attack in 2013.

[38] Mike Bailey: Wolves midfielder 1966-77, played with Graham and wrote newspaper column. Family reported his dementia diagnosis in 2020.

[39] Wayne Clarke: younger brother of Graham's childhood team-mate Allan Clarke, and Wolves striker (1978-84) under Graham.

[40] Ron Flowers: member of 1966 World Cup-winning squad, Graham's hero and role model in his early career at Wolves. Died 2021.

[41] Gerry Harris: Wolves left-back 1953-66 and senior player when Graham signed as an apprentice. Died 2020.

[42] John McAlle: Wolves centre-back 1967-81. Became landscape gardener when retired from football.

[43] Willie Carr: Wolves midfielder 1975-82, first player to be sold by Wolves' receivers in 1982 (£10,000 to Millwall), just before Graham's appointment as manager.

[44] Keith Downing: Wolves midfielder 1987-93, played under Graham Turner.

[45] Fred Kemp: Wolves Apprentice and contemporary of Graham's in 1961, first-team player 1963-65.

Printed in Great Britain
by Amazon